PETALUMA'S
POULTRY PIONEERS

A REUNION PHOTOGRAPH OF FORMER EMPLOYEES OF POULTRY PRODUCERS OF CENTRAL CALIFORNIA: (FROM LEFT) MARILYN HANSEN, EMMA BRANSEN SONKSEN, HILDA TIEMANN KEEHN, ANNE FIGUEIRA PETERSON, ALEXIS DAY AND VERNA VOGLE.

PHOTOGRAPH BY LAKIN KHAN © 1993

PETALUMA'S POULTRY PIONEERS

Recall the Heyday of Chicken Ranching

THEA S. LOWRY, EDITOR

Manifold Press
ROSS, CALIFORNIA
Under the Auspices of
The Petaluma Museum Association

Printed in the United States of America

Manifold Press

Ross, California 94957

Ordering information page 127

Library of Congress Catalog Card Number 93-78245

ISBN 0-9610116-0-2

FOREWORD

Don't let anyone try to sell you on the idea that growing up on a chicken farm was a barrel of fun. Perhaps you'll find a few rays of sunshine in this collection of memories by those who lived during that era when Petaluma was The World's Egg Basket. But the message that emerges is that working on a chicken ranch was hard repetitive labor seven days a week. For the youngsters it was chores before you went to school, chores when you came home from school, and chores every weekend.

However, as owner and keeper of the flock, you made the decisions, watched grain prices, determined feeding regimens, negotiated with the hatcheries and egg brokers, battled infestation and disease, and managed the business in the great tradition of American free enterprise. In spite of it all, independence and pride shine through in many of these reminiscences.

The golden days of the chicken ranch began just before the turn of the century and lasted to the 1940s when a nation at war needed all the eggs and chickens it could get. Peaks were reached in the late teens, mid-20s and late 30s. The decline was abrupt in the 1950s as mega-farms and technology made the Petaluma-style egg business obsolete.

These recollections by industry participants were collected by volunteers in the Chicken House Project, a program of the Petaluma Museum. They are pure documents in that little editing was done, just some words added or subtracted to smooth out the text. The genuine flavor remains unsullied.

Tangible evidence of the business still exists in the weathered, collapsing chicken houses of southern Sonoma County. Some of them have been converted or spruced up into sturdier structures and now serve other purposes. But most are hollow shells slowly disappearing under the twin onslaughts of weather and neglect. This anthology will outlast the architectural remnants.

Jud Snyder

INTRODUCTION

A lmost exactly a century ago Petaluma got interested in raising chickens. Poultrymen formed their first society in 1889 with Lyman Byce at the helm, A.A. Armstrong as secretary and Chris Nisson, treasurer. Three years later, Chris Nisson had the Petaluma Incubator Company build him a 2,000-egg incubator, the largest known at the time. People traveled long distances to see it, and worried that "there would be too many chickens." In 1893 Nisson shipped "100 chx to G.T. Webster of Schellville @ 8c each." In 1894, Nisson, a thoughtful and conscientious rancher, published a booklet of advice on incubation specially adapted for the West Coast. About the same time, George Lasher opened a hatchery in the family home. Over the next few decades Petaluma dominated the West Coast poultry industry and achieved world acclaim....Then, one by one, the family farms failed.

Dilapidated chicken houses, fading into the pastures, gave mute evidence of a changed economy. In the 1970s I began photographing the lichen-encrusted, delightfully rachitic, teetering structures with their swaybacked rooflines and sagging window frames. In 1986, I started to research a book about the eighty-year reign of the White Leghorn.

No amount of squinting at microfilm, however, can rival the immediacy of first-hand accounts from industry families. Responding to a call for volunteers, Maxine Kortum Durney and several others conducted interviews and collected biographical sketches. Condensed and edited, these stories illuminate an era when integrity, loyalty, hard work and thrift were the hallmarks of character.

Thea S. Lowry

PREFACE

It was as though we had touched a wellspring of private sentiment, long buried under some notion that others viewed the farms and the industry as unimportant and slightly amusing: Chicken feathers! Manure! Chick sexing! Egg Day!

Yet Petaluma was international: farm families came from Scandinavia, eastern and western Europe, Russia and Japan, and what emerged is anecdotal, personal, detailed and sometimes humorous. Impressive above all is the respect for the rigorous life. Pride is evident in the scenes recalled of grain barges from the Delta, grain trains from the Midwest, and grain trucks from the Valley. Images persist of the clean, white, fresh eggs, shipped downriver on the steamers, on trucks and railway cars; of meatbirds on their way to San Francisco and the East Coast, and baby chicks in special boxes being sent all over the West and Midwest.

To all these storytellers, I am grateful, and to those who collected the stories; to Thea Lowry, who knew the personal histories were extraordinary; and to Nancy Bauer, of the Petaluma Museum, who helped keep the project on track.

Maxine Kortum Durney

GOOD EGGS: ACKNOWLEDGEMENTS

Members of The Chicken House Project: Marilyn Bragdon, Heimer Carlson, Maxine Kortum Durney, Richard Hensley, Lakin Khan and Jud Snyder. Nancy Bauer, Liaison; Thea S. Lowry, Director.

Supporters: Prue Draper, Ruby Eatherton, Karen Eberhardt, Herb Graff, Anna Harrigan, Cheryl Jern, Paloma Luce, Phillip Naftaly, Mary Nakagawa, Lucille Taapken and Martha Wohletz.

Acknowledgements: Special thanks to Dr. Francine Bradley and Ed Mannion, for generous use of their archives; *Also* Walter Bragdon, Mert Doss, Cort Fernald, Ed Fratini, Jo Ann Garlington, Jim Heig, Lewis A. Hillyard, Lucy Kortum, Gaye LeBaron, Dick Lieb, Michael Mannion, Robert Mannion, Charles Nelson, Kiyo Okazaki, Bill Soberanes, Asana Tamaras, Baron Wolman, The American Poultry Historical Society, Petaluma *Argus-Courier*, Petaluma Library, Santa Rosa *Press Democrat*.

Sponsors and Donors: Leon Barlas, Clifton Buck-Kauffman, Ruby Eatherton, Wilfred Lieb, Paloma Luce, Steve Mahrt, Richard Marson, The Petaluma Museum Association, Petaluma Chamber of Commerce for the Transient Occupancy Tax Fund, Sonoma County Historical Society, the Pacific Egg and Poultry Association, Sonoma County Landmarks Commission, Steve Tomasini, Renée Vences de Marson, Richard Weber and Richard J. Werthimer.

Editor's Note: My thanks to the members of the Chicken House Project for their generous, patient and conscientious work. I am especially grateful to the narrators who came forward to share their experiences with us. I accept responsiblity for summarizing and retelling their stories as they appear here. The interviews were collected by Maxine Kortum Durney unless otherwise noted.

Thea S. Lowry, *Editor*

CONTENTS & CONTRIBUTORS

INDEX TO TITLES

QUALITY CHICKS SINCE 1899

He had left his Ohio home seven years before. George Amial Lasher was 23 when he started a chicken business at Fort Bidwell in Modoc County, California. Although he had never seen an artificial incubator, in 1883 he constructed a successful device for hatching chicken eggs and thereafter called it his "brain child."

After a decade of struggling to survive, George decided to relocate. He loaded a covered wagon with his household goods, including the incubator, and brought his family to Sonoma County. With his wife Nora, two daughters under three, and leading a cow tied behind the wagon, they camped along the trail eight weeks, arriving in Petaluma during a furious storm three days after Christmas, 1893.

They bought a house on the west side of town and converted one room into a hatchery. The incubator had a five gallon water tank attached to the side, heated by kerosene, which kept the temperature at 102° F for twenty-one days. The fertile eggs were carefully turned twice a day. Advertised as "George Lasher the Chicken Hatcher," its phone number was "Black-1331." In those days the exchange on the west side of town was Black and the east side exchange was White.

They soon had four children and a thriving business. The Lashers raised several fancy breeds and won prizes with them at the poultry shows.

Their advertisements ran:

LEADING VARIETIES OF DAY OLD CHICKS
FURNISHED ALL SEASONS OF THE YEAR.
THOROUGHBRED RHODE ISLAND REDS, ANCONAS,
BUFF LANGSHAN, PLYMOUTH ROCK AND LEGHORNS

In February, 1898, Alaska gold fever struck George. He arranged for his family to return to Fort Bidwell to stay with Nora's parents, and headed north.

His first strike, a gold nugget, was preserved as a stickpin and later a tie tack. His dreams of riches from the Seward Peninsula, however, didn't materialize so he—and hundreds of other disappointed miners—returned on the final sailing of the season during the fall of 1899.

The Lashers returned to their Petaluma poultry business. Their new brick hatchery building was considered a model and soon their trade flourished. Nora wrote, "We will soon be quite busy in our hatching business. We have orders on the books for 77,800 chicks to be hatched between now and the end of March. Several thousand have already been put out and orders are still coming in for April and May."

In 1917 the uninsured hatchery was gutted by fire. More than 1600 baby chicks and 15,000 high grade hatching eggs were lost and 100 incubators destroyed or damaged. When it was rebuilt, the owners installed a mammoth Kandy Incubator, capable of holding 40,000 eggs at one time. This gave the hatchery the capacity of 140,000 eggs, making it one of the largest hatcheries in Sonoma County. In 1923, while it was still successful, George sold the hatchery.

The family lived for a while in the Healdsburg area where the plentiful deer made Nora famous for her venison mincemeat. George Lasher died ten years later at age 73.

*Research by **Lois Lasher** [died 1985]*
*Compiled by **Barbara Lasher***
*Contributed by **Patreece Mellars***

SCENE IN LASHER'S HATCHERY— 1912 PHOTO BY A.J. FREEMAN FROM PETALUMA MUSEUM

THREE KINDS OF CHICKEN HOUSES

My parents were in the poultry business in Cotati and Stony Point in 1912.

There were three main kinds of chicken houses. First were the brooder houses where the baby chicks lived, warmed by a heater which was at first coal and later gas-powered.

Then there were the colony houses, especially in the Two Rock area where they had free range. These small houses could be towed by a team of horses to a new location.

The regular chicken houses were "floor operations," with dropping boards below the roosts that needed to be cleaned once a week.

Interview by Thea Lowry   *Paul Hantzche*

DORIS GERE IN DAD'S 1927 MODEL T FORD, WITH "10 CASES OF EGGS FOR PPCC OR SALES' HATCHERY." PHOTO BY RAYMOND T. GERE OF HESSEL. SEE PAGE 109

ONCE WE WENT TO PORTLAND

My parents both came from Norway. My father shipped out as a cabin boy when he was 17 with a captain who was his brother-in-law. He wound up as a fireman in Portland, Oregon, where he met my mother. She worked for a wealthy family, the Meiers of the Meier and Frank's department store in Portland.

My folks heard about Petaluma and decided to try it. They bought five acres on time, with a little house that had been a granary attached to the tank house.

Every day after school, I changed into an old dress—no overalls for girls in those days. I cleaned eggs. First we washed the eggs, then sandpapered every speck, and we always packed the eggs with the little end down. Once, when I was four, we went to Portland. It was the only trip we ever took.

Later the house was enlarged and moved closer to the road, where it is now, on Skillman Lane.

Virginia Hansen Miller

ONE DAY MY MOTHER
SEWED UP THE DOG

My parents came from Europe with nothing but their suitcases. My father was a machinist and made two or three dollars a day. Some people made only a dollar a day.

When they bought this house on Willow Lane in Cotati it was only half this size. They built that back room on, that's where I was born. We had a well-house with a windmill on top which lifted the water up to the storage tank. When the tank was full you put the brake on the windmill. Gravity supplied the pressure.

In the old days when you moved they sent a wagon and a team. They loaded the furniture up and they pulled the wagon down to the steamer —*Gold,* I guess it was, and they pulled the wagon on the boat and then the horses stayed in San Francisco. When they arrived in Petaluma they'd pull the wagon off again with a couple of horses and bring it up to the ranch and unload the furniture.

We went to Petaluma maybe only once or twice a month, not twice a day like people do today. As a kid I got up early and did the ranch work here as you never had nothing to do; you were always looking for more to do. You had to become a jack-of-all-trades. If you had to pay everybody to do something, you wouldn't have anything left. Yes, the farmer is a plumber and a carpenter and an electrician.

I walked from here to school in Penngrove along the railroad tracks. It was more than two miles by road or about a mile and a block by way of the tracks. The roads were all

dirt around here and in Marin County until probably the
'30s. Some of my friends and I used to sneak off from
school and go down to the creek and go swimming and then
we'd time it to get back to school as the lunch hour ended.
We did that for a few weeks and finally the teachers asked,
"What's the matter with you? How come you're wet?"

When I was a kid I worked in the prune packing plant or
would help neighbors clean chicken houses.

We used to buy grain—sacks of wheat and barley—
bring them to the barn and stack them 10, 12 foot
high. Later on we'd bring them up to the bins and dump it
in. This was before they had bulk feed.

We had brooder houses. We'd buy the chicks, a thousand or
fifteen hundred, sometimes three thousand, and we'd keep
them warm with heaters and then when they were about
three months old, we'd move them down to these bigger
houses.

The colony houses had maybe 50 birds, built on 2x8s.
Colony houses had a hole drilled in each end of them and
you'd hitch a team to move them when there was a lot of
dirt under them, so you didn't need to clean them, just pull
them to another spot. Built on a sled.

Just cleaning and grading the eggs, you put them on the egg
scale—extra large, large, medium and small—before we
took them down to be sold. It took my mother pretty near a
third of the day, to brush them by hand or wipe them with a
wet cloth. We'd come and help her out if we didn't have
anything else to do.

My mother made us some toys. She'd take a sock and fill it
up with cotton and sew a couple of eyes on it and a nose

and a mouth: a doll. You played with those kinds of toys.

One time the horse kicked my dog and made a big gash in his leg. My mother got a needle and thread and sewed it up and the dog was OK. But the chickens, they'd get chickenpox and they got bronchitis and you lost sometimes near half of them.

My parents got their first horseless carriage in 1922 and then a Model T in 1924. The front house was built in 1927. We still kept the horse for plowing and ranch work, but we never took him on the road anymore.

One time I was helping my dad start the truck by hand cranking when it kicked and broke my arm. I grabbed my arm and set it already and when we got to the doctor he said it was set perfect and so he just put a cast around it. We did a lot of our own doctoring.

In the Depression families were so poor, you didn't get help from the county or the government. Sometimes the wife and kids moved in with her folks and the husband went out to look for work or he went out as a hobo. There was a hobo camp down by the creek near the railroad tracks. They'd go around begging for food just to survive. Or they'd work on little county projects for a dollar a day. Board and room and a dollar a day.

I guess we finally decided to get rid of the horse in 1948, when we got the first tractor.

Jack Haberer

INTERVIEW BY MIRIAM HUTCHINS

TURNING EGGS FOR SUCCESS

My parents, Henry and Anna Graff, originally planned to settle in Ukiah when they arrived in California in 1900, but when my mother heard that the population was mostly Indian (she had sad memories of the past Indian wars in Minnesota), they stayed in Petaluma. My father bought about twenty acres on Corona Road, with a house, a barn and three apricot trees. One neighbor had a big adobe house with a large cellar underneath where General Vallejo's Indians stored potatoes after harvest.

Leo Bourke invented an incubator and gave his first model to my father to try out. It was a tiny one, holding a dozen eggs and heated by a kerosene lamp. My father put it in the bathtub in case it might explode. The eggs were turned over by hand twice a day like hens do and, right on schedule, twelve chicks hatched. That was the beginning of Bourke's Must Hatch company.

Then Mr. L.C. Byce perfected an incubator too, and soon my father had a large incubator house with Byce incubators installed. They were smaller and easier to operate.

My brother, sister and I would arise at 4:00 AM every morning and turn eggs before going to school and again after coming home. I calculated that I turned over one million eggs.

Father sold the chicks to ranchers all over the valley and some out of state. Our hatchery, the Success Poultry Ranch, prospered for years. My father and A. R. Coulsen perfected a well-balanced feed mixture and manufactured it in downtown Petaluma.

I remember the 1906 Earthquake; it didn't do much damage, but we slept outdoors afterwards. I remember standing on the road and seeing the sky red at night from the San Francisco Fire. I remember the time in 1911 when Fred Wiseman flew his air mail trip between Petaluma and Santa Rosa. He landed down in the field near Corona Road about where the new fire station now stands. We all ran down to see the plane.

Fishing boats used to dock on the river and my folks used to rush down and buy fresh herring in season.

My parents bought me a racehorse when I was about ten. I used to drive myself to town when *Perils of Pauline* was playing and tie my horse at the hitching rail. I spent many happy hours at the Kenilworth Park race track, and I also belonged to the Senior Riding Club.

Now there are so many new neighbors. The hayfields from here to town are disappearing and homes occupy the land.

[DIED, AGED 90, JANUARY 1989—ED.]   By *Ida A. McDaniel*

CHILDREN LILLIEBELL, IDA AND EARL WITH HENRY AND ANNA GRAFF, C. 1914.
PHOTO COURTESY HERB GRAFF.

CHRISTMAS PRESENTS

My father, Albert Larsen, was from Denmark. My mother, Gertrude Anderton, was born here and her mother lived in Petaluma. My dad was a very hard working poultryman and he also raised fox terrier dogs and sold them in San Francisco at Robinson's. We also had a hired hand who took his meals with us but had his own house.

We took one vacation trip my entire childhood. My parents and grandparents planned to see the Olympic Games in Los Angeles, about 1932, but we never got past Santa Cruz. My dad and grandpa went deep sea fishing and were overcome with seasickness and stopped right there.

Christmas time was always financially hard for us. The cold weather affected the hens' laying and the price of eggs would be down, perhaps ten cents a dozen. I would be lucky to get a lunch box with crayons.

One year I remember I got a beautiful doll I had seen in Tomasini's Hardware. She had a pink dress. My cousin (whose father was an affluent butcher) got the same doll in a yellow dress. My parents sacrificed to get the six dollars for that doll. I've never forgotten how happy that doll made me.

By *Althea Larsen Torliatt*

CHICKEN RANCH CHILDHOOD

O ur place was a small one and my father never needed to hire outside labor. Growing up, my services were needed and expected. I was a chicken ranch child from 1908 to 1918.

Every year we'd plant a couple of acres in kale. My father would line out the rows with a cord, dig a hole with a spade and I'd insert the plant; he'd close the hole with his foot and we moved along briskly, row upon row. We picked the lower kale leaves daily and put them in the engine-driven kale-cutter to feed to the chickens. I was never allowed to help with the kale-cutter.

My main task was to clean, weigh, sort and pack eggs into wooden cases to go to town twice a week. We worked on the bottom floor of the tankhouse, hearing the sound of the motor pumping water from the well below up to the tank above. It never occurred to me to resent the task of "doing" the eggs, and once, when I was careless and broke too many, I was relieved of my job and felt absolutely desolated until I was reinstated.

Another task was to chop kindling and carry wood daily to feed the kitchen stove which was for cooking and heating water. Our food was kept fresh in an evaporative cooler which was a screened frame draped with with burlap sacks kept wet from a water container on top. Our cooler was set under a cherry tree; our butter never melted and was always spreadable. It was simple, efficient and never needed repair. That same cherry tree supported the flapping body of the weekly beheaded chicken. It was immersed in scalding water, and the feathers removed quickly; I learned early on to eviscerate the bird.

We raised much of the food for our table ourselves with our small orchard and a well-tended vegetable garden. We kept cucumbers and melons cool by placing them under a wet gunny sack at the foot of our fine oak tree. Squash, potatoes, onions and apples were individually wrapped and placed in straw for keeping over the winter. We canned vegetables and fruit and kept staples on hand since we went to town by horse and wagon only twice a week. Our horse was called Wash after Uncle Washington who left Dad a little money.

Every Monday the family's clothes were washed in a tub with someone turning a handle that rotated its wooden paddles. Someone needed to carry hot water from the stove to the washer. It drained into the vegetable garden. White clothes were boiled on the stove and all of the clothes were hung on the line to dry. At first we did not have any water piped into the house and we were all immensely pleased when cold water was finally piped to the sink. Tuesday was ironing day. We used irons with detachable handles heated on the stove.

Saturday was bath night. We took turns stepping into a galvanized tub brought into the kitchen, set next to the stove and filled with hot water. My father bathed last. The family used a privy behind the feed house and a chamber pot was under each bed. The privy was treated with lime and had to be cleaned out yearly. Dad said he needed alcoholic courage for that job.

We had to clean and fill the kerosene lamps each morning. Dad's reading light was special, as it had a mantle and gave a white light. It was a great day when electricity came to our lane and into our house. A single cord hung from the center of the ceiling in each room and an unshaded bulb gave us marvelous light with no lamps to bother with. One day curiosity overcame me and I stuck a silver butter knife into an empty socket. My lesson was instantaneous—but no one could ever fathom what put the nick in the edge of the butter knife.

I walked the 3/4 mile to school down a sandy lane, carrying my lunch in a fine tobacco tin with a hinged cover. Our horse grazed in the driveway and terrified me when I came home from school as occasionally he would take out after me. Our gate had an automatic opening device a local man named Johnson invented. When the wagon wheel ran over a bar in the driveway it tripped a lever that opened and later closed the gate. We could never understand why everyone didn't have this device.

When I was ten or eleven, Dad bought the first Ford in the lane. It had one seat with a bonnet to protect the driver and in back a rack was bolted to the frame to hold the cases of eggs. We could replace the rack with another seat and take a picnic basket and Sunday afternoon drives, and it was easier to drive to town. We kept Wash for plowing and harrowing and for hauling feed around the ranch.

In those days merchants opened for business at 8:00 AM. Once I rode to town with my father as a special treat—he'd conduct business and stop for a drink usually—and he bought me a hat. The crown was black patent leather and the brim of black and white checked fabric. I purely loved that headpiece!

Anna Keyes Neilsen

SEE ALSO PAGE 43

THEY CAME ON THE STEAMER GOLD

My parents, Hans Larsen and Anna Lund, came from Denmark. They came to Petaluma on the steamer *Gold,* to become partners in George Knudsen's chicken ranch on Marshall Avenue.

As a child, we didn't take vacations. Picnics, yes, but we had to get home to feed the chickens and milk the cow before dark. Sometimes the men would leave the picnic to go home to perform these chores, then return, if it were a long summer evening. During the school year, when I got home from Cinnabar School, I'd change clothes and run out to spend as much time as I could working in my garden before it was time to gather and pack eggs.

I had three houses to gather eggs from. One was next to the neighbor's pig farm. Pigs draw rats and my father would go down there at night to shoot them. I was terrified to go in that one to gather eggs and was always relieved when I finished there. Before packing the eggs, we separated the clean from the dirty and sandpapered the dirty. We learned to pick up four eggs at a time in each hand for the packing. If we didn't finish the cleaning and packing before dinner, we went on to our homework after dinner and Dad finished the eggs.

My brother and I would show off by swinging buckets of eggs round and round, using centrifugal force to keep the eggs from falling out.

When my father bought a new car, he converted the old sedan into a little truck. He cut out the back seat and built a platform to haul eggs and feed. He never bought a regular pickup.

Betty Larsen Fraser

RECOLLECTIONS OF A PETALUMA FARM CHILDHOOD

K restin Krestensen Skjødt, my father, came from Denmark in 1905. His method was to alternate chicken yards to grow vegetables for the family and corn for both the family and the chickens. The chickens had the run of only one yard.

My brother and I had to pick kale for the chickens every morning before school. I hated to go to school with kale stains under my fingernails. We would push the big leaves and stalks into the electric kale cutter, which my father taught us to use. He showed us the threshold beyond which our fingers were not to go. He felt if we learned to respect it when we were young we would have no accidents later. There were many children in the Petaluma schools who were missing ends of fingers, and sometimes whole fingers.

Gophers loved the kale. You sometimes saw a whole plant disappear, pulled underground, in front of your eyes. My brother and I were paid a few cents for each gopher we caught, a rare source of our own income for us farm kids.

When I was old enough to gather eggs I learned to move slowly, watching to see if there were any "broody" hens in the nests. I was scared of the the broody hens and would try not to startle any of the others. I dreaded the great upheaval if one bird became frightened, because then all would fly off the nests, scolding and squawking, stirring up a great amount of dust. Later I learned I was allergic to the dust, and was excused from gathering eggs. I worked in the garden instead.

My father performed autopsies on some of the birds to determine the cause of death. Sometimes he would take it to the Chicken Pharmacy for their opinion. We tried many kinds of vaccines and capsules to prevent diseases. I hated those days when we had to catch chickens–smelly things!– and vaccinate under one wing, and force a pill down their throats. When they died they were sold to the "dead man" who picked them up from a barrel at the foot of the driveway once a week.

The chickens were fed oyster shells to provide calcium for strong eggshells. We had a big bin of oyster shells where we children loved to play and to search for whole shells. They were brought up the Petaluma River on barges and scow schooners from South San Francisco, where they were dredged from the bottom of the Bay.

To provide a longer day and therefore encourage more laying, farmers would provide artificial light to the hens. My father's system depended on an alarm clock which tripped a switch and turned the lights on.

We kept 2,000 hens in three main chicken houses, each 100 feet long. They were built by a carpenter named Carl Engel after we moved to Bodega Avenue from our Sonoma Mountain place in the mid 1920s.

Before a new flock of young chickens was moved from the brooder house into one of the large chicken houses, the house was emptied of old birds. They were sold as meat birds. The house was then thoroughly cleaned of old straw and manure and hand-sprayed with diesel oil to control fleas and lice. The roosts were sprayed with "Black Leaf-40," a tobacco derivative. We spread straw on the floor and put rice hulls in the nests.

Ruby Scott Eatherton

FARM BOY

The farm was in Two Rock Valley with a house, barn and sheds all made of hand-hewn lumber. There was no electricity, no radio, no television, no running water nor hot water tank and, of course, no telephone.

Water was scarce; you went to the well and lowered a bucket and drank from the dipper. All the water used in the kitchen and for washing was carefully saved, and what was left after washing dishes or bathing was used to water the garden. Mother cooked on a wood stove which also heated our water for bathing in the wooden tub in the kitchen. Clothes were washed by hand on a washboard.

We made our own butter—there were no creameries in those days—in a hand-turned churn, and sold the excess. Almost all of our food was produced on the farm: apples, pears, plums, potatoes, pumpkins, carrots, turnips, peas, beans, beets, cabbage; and we fattened a pig or two every year. We canned and dried fruit for winter use and made jams and jellies; we sold extra potatoes and currants and used the money to buy flour, sugar, salt, pepper and rice and sometimes fresh meat. Our transportation was afoot, horseback or horse and buggy. For light we used candles and kerosene lamps.

When I was very little, we were slaughtering a sheep for mutton. I was terrified of its peculiar eyes. After the sheep was killed, I said to my grandfather Eric in Danish, "Grandpa, I am not afraid of a sheep." I heard about this for many, many years.

I remember my little brother Peter: I was not yet four years old and I can still see my mother pacing up and down with him in her arms, kissing him and calling out endearments to him, but little Peter did not hear her nor was he conscious of her love; the child had died of whooping cough. Mother had five children in ten years; we were ten miles from the nearest doctor with no phones nor automobiles.

B efore the year was out, my mother had died herself. She was kind to me and very nice to hug, but she was gone before I was five years old so I do not remember her very well. The funeral was in the spring and whenever I smell lilacs, I recall the the little churchyard and the people gathered about my mother's grave.

[Sonoma County Death Records: *"Nisson, Ingeborg. Born 1848, Died March 18, 1887. Buried at Two Rock Church."* -Ed.]

My two older sisters started school before I did, and began to learn English as we spoke only Danish at home. When I was six I started school. My teacher gave me a notebook and a pencil. He was astonished when I wrote the whole alphabet in it which I had learned from my sisters.

All over our clothes were homemade; some from homespun cloth brought from Denmark. Every year my grandmother made me two suits of jackets and pants and knitted my stockings of wool: two pairs, knee length, and they lasted all year. I didn't have long pants until I was twelve.

Our entertainment was playing in the barn and the orchard, the currant patch and the fields. We had horses and dogs and calves and we played Hide and Seek. We had a swing in the trees and I had a tricycle.

W e usually had two dogs; an older dog to do the chores and a younger one learning the business. A dog's chores are many and varied on a ranch: the cows have to be brought in for milking and all kinds of stray

CHICKEN PHARMACIST WATSON M. MCFADDEN AND CUSTOMER.
1942 PHOTO BY RUSSELL LEE, WHO NOTED, *"PETALUMA A TOWN OF 8000."*
COURTESY OF THE LIBRARY OF CONGRESS ~ SEE ALSO PAGES 11 AND 43.

animals—cows, pigs, neighbors' horses—chased back to where they belong. A dog keeps the cats in their place, chases the chickens off the porch and out of the garden, and acts as a general policeman.

One year we had a lot of rats and the ranch dogs couldn't cope with them. A rat dog is a specialist so we got a Skye terrier, full grown, to do this job. He was so hairy you couldn't tell whether he was coming or going. His face was completely covered with long hair, but he could see a rat and catch it. Whenever we moved a chicken house he would stand by trembling with eagerness, and when the rats came into view he would spring into action like a fire-cracker. He would work all day digging and tearing up boards around a pile of lumber trying to get at a rat.

He had two major ambitions besides the killing of rats: to dig out a gopher and to run down a rabbit. There is no record of a dog ever digging up a gopher and our ranch dogs knew that. They would sniff at the burrow and dig a few licks and quit, but the Skye would dig all day until he was completely underground. He would come up for air once in while with his face covered with dirt and his paws practically worn out, and then he would resume his labors. He never did catch a gopher.

He'd also chase jackrabbits. They didn't mind; it was mild and invigorating exercise for them. The Skye was dead serious about it, but the rabbit would sit up and comb his whiskers while he waited for the Skye to catch up.

There was a rabbit in the corn field that the Skye would chase on his days off. He could never get the rabbit out of the corn field for the rabbit simply switched rows and ran back and forth, or sauntered, rather, for he never had to hurry. Nevertheless, the Skye put in a lot of time and almost ran his heart out in hopes that he would get that insolent rabbit and, strangely enough, he did.

Our number two dog was a foolish young shepherd who would join the Skye on his adventures. One day he was helping in the cornfield and the rabbit, as usual, was running up and down the rows, but he got mixed up somehow, on account of the two dogs, and ran head first into the Skye, who killed him. Right now. I had been a spectator and went over to congratulate the Skye as he worried and tossed the dead rabbit, but he resented the intrusion and bit me. He raised a terrrible ruckus when the shepherd came near. When evening came, he hauled the rabbit back in the corn field and buried it.

I used to go out in the fields with the hired men when I was little and ride home at noon on a big work horse. Once when we were haying, I was on top of the load of hay when the load slipped and fell off with me under it. I was scared but not hurt, for the men got the hay off me in a hurry before I smothered. Another time I was run over by a sled and got a big cut on my head which bled profusely and created a big stir in the house.

The hired man's wages were $25 a month and "found"– three meals a day and a bed in the bunkhouse; they furnished their own blankets. When I was a little older I worked as a hired hand at a dairy; those men put in 16-hour days except Sundays when they only had to milk their string of 25 cows twice. Other days they worked in the fields, fixed fences, plowed, hoed plants, etc., from 3:45 AM until about 8 PM. The bunkhouse was furnished with a metal basin, soap and a roller towel. There were no toilets and, at one place, not even an outside privy; we used the barn. There was no shower so some men bathed once a week in the horse trough;

others waited until summer to bathe in a pond or creek.

One wouldn't think that on $300 a year that any of the hired men could get anywhere, but many did. They saved their wages until they had enough to rent a small place and little by little became well off. I know dozens of men who came to this country with no more than their clothes who became wealthy farmers after starting as a "hired man" at $25 a month.

At one point, we had an Indian hired man named Juan Butcher Knife. His wife was Marie Baking Powder and she did our washing every Monday. One Monday, Marie didn't show up and Juan told us in mixed Spanish, Indian and English that Marie was having a baby but would come tomorrow. She did come Tuesday with the infant all wrapped up and in a basket. She hung the bundle in a tree and went on with the wash, taking time out now and then to nurse her baby.

By *Eric A. Nisson (1881-1964)*   COURTESY ODILE NISSON ROCHE
Son of Christopher Nisson, industry founder
and pioneer hatchery man, 1848-1904.

ERIC NISSON WITH "OLD NUMBER ONE," HIS FATHER'S 2000-EGG CAPACITY INCUBATOR BUILT IN 1890. PHOTO BY ROLAND A. HARTMAN, 1951.

THE RIDE TO TOWN

My parents were born in Germany and came to San Francisco before the turn of the century. The devastation of the 1906 Earthquake led to their move to Petaluma, where they first rented a small chicken ranch in the Liberty District, and then purchased a 14 acre ranch from my uncle in 1912. It had colony houses, a granary, barn, wagon shed, egg room and a five room residence. There were eight of us children.

Every spring we purchased 1,500 unsexed baby chicks from the Pioneer Hatchery. In the fall, the hens were culled to make room for the pullets. We had between 4 and 5,000 laying hens at all times. We loaded the horse and wagon with cases of eggs to be delivered to the Poultry Producers each morning, a five mile trip that took one hour. My father would take a couple of us children at a time, always exciting. At the bridge over Willow Creek on Stony Point we'd watch the turtles dive into the water. Another place had no culvert and at high tide the horses had to ford a shallow waterway, and this was fun for us kids.

What is now the Eagles Hall was originally the Cinnabar School and it was the halfway mark to town. After dropping off the eggs and picking up empty cases, we loaded up with feed. They had ice water at the mill, and it was always a treat. When we shopped for groceries the owner gave us peanuts and the butcher treated us to a chunk of bologna or a frankfurter while he chatted with my father.

My father bought grain in bulk from the Golden Eagle Milling Company and mixed it with a hoe in a big trough.

This was before the time of the mechanical mixers. Our place was near Liberty Station on the railroad. The train went by at 3:00 PM and that was a signal to the chickens. They all flocked to the gate to be fed. We had this routine: first we had our coffee, then the train came, then we fed the chickens and gathered the eggs.

The ranch is gone now. Now it's the Liberty Golf Course.

Hilda Tiemann Keehn   SEE ALSO PAGE 31

THIRTY~FOUR ACRES NEAR COTATI

My grandfather, August Grube, was born in Germany and my grandmother, Hannah Marie Lawson, was born in Denmark. They married in 1889 and came to Sonoma County in 1894 and bought land. It started out raw but he was diligent and made a comfortable home, sturdy chicken houses, a barn, orchard and wells. My grandfather kept about 2,500 hens. He was one of the enterprising poultrymen of the district and a member of the Central California Poultry Producers Association. Eventually it was thirty-four acres near Cotati. My grandmother was active in her church and enjoyed gardening. Both grandparents died before World War II was over.

Together they reared six sons and one daughter.

By **Miranda Scannell**

PULLETS BY NIGHT

My parents, who were from Austria and Germany, bought a ranch on Skillman Lane about 1922 and began to raise chickens. As a child, I helped to cull the flock, and to move the pullets from the brooder house to the chicken house when they became pullets. We carried them by hand, at night, six at a time. Later we used coops to move them. I remember picking kale for them.

In the Depression my mother went to work to help support the family; first in the laundry at the Petaluma Hotel, then at Poultry Producers, candling eggs. My father went into the sack business. I sewed the holes in the sacks and was paid a penny for each one I did.

Gretchen Stonitsch Lichau

A RACE AGAINST THE EGGS

I was born in 1911 and went to first grade at Stony Point. My parents had come from Denmark around 1908, had four children and ran a chicken ranch in Bloomfield with 4,000 chickens.

My mother died when I was twelve. A few years later we bought our place on Wiegand Hill, which used to be a road-house before Prohibition and it still had its bar when we moved there. The ranch was 72 acres with four big chicken houses as well as colony houses. We had 6,500 chickens.

It fell to me to be the cook but I didn't prepare the food the way Mother had. I did the cleaning and washing on Saturdays and later, when I was invited to a football game, I had to have the game explained to me.

I had my own horse, and one day my cousin and I went up the hill to gather eggs. I was riding and he was driving the farm horse and pulling the wagon. When we finished the egg gathering I challenged him to a race. "A race against the eggs," we called it later. Off we went, down the hill. Imagine what happened to the eggs. We lost the day's gathering but my father must have been amused. He didn't scold.

During the Depression, we traded potatoes for canned food and haircuts. Indians came to dig potatoes every August. They put up tents and I remember the smell of their campfires and going down to their camp and talking to them. After high school and business college, I went to work for the Poultry Producers in 1932 for $11 for my six-day week. I was a clerk in the Egg Department preparing egg tags. I got married and was away for ten years, but came back and went to work in the feed department. I worked there until 1968.

Emma Bransen Sonksen

EARLY EGG DAY PARADE. FROM FARM ADVISOR FILES,
COURTESY DR. FRANCINE A. BRADLEY, AVIAN SCIENCES, UC-DAVIS.

THE KING RANCH

My grandfather, Joaquin Coelho, was born in the Azores in the early 1800s and was a whaler by trade. The lure of gold brought him to California during the Rush and he earned a small fortune working the Argonaut Mine in Jackson and a quartz mine partnership in Drytown. His friends of that era started calling him King (a play on Joaquin) and, for all practical purposes, Joaquin became John Joseph King. In the 1850s, John took his earnings and purchased forty acres in the Rancho La Miseraria tract fronting Bodega Avenue outside of Petaluma.

At first, John's time was spent building a house and raising produce for the San Francisco market. The house soon became a home to five children, with additional rooms added as the years passed. My father, the youngest, was born there in 1873. He met my mother, born in Germany, when she came to the ranch to pick fruit at age 17.

When the market for pears failed, my grandfather started raising chickens. My father, John Jr., inherited the ranch. I can remember being an active participant as a girl in the many duties of ranch life, especially every aspect of raising chickens from the time they came out of the boxes as darling chicks. In those days they were immediately put in a room around a warm hover, which was like a big metal umbrella. There they were cared for until they became pullets, and subsequently moved to laying houses. In 1921 my father had 10,000 chickens. He was good at culling a flock and his advice was often sought in identifying the best laying hens.

Needless to say, poultry ranching took its toll on our social life. At gatherings, when everybody else began to pull out the goodies for the second feast of the day, my father would say, "C'mon, kids, time to go home and gather the eggs." We used big heavy, willow baskets that lasted for years. Father would come around to the brooder houses driving our old plug, which is what you call a no-good horse, and he'd pick up the eggs we'd collected and take them to the egg house, where we had to clean them by hand in cold water and pack them. If we accidentally cracked an egg, we children would throw it out the window. Once in a while my father would find one and we'd be in real trouble.

It was hard, hard work, and we never got through. At dusk we'd go into the house, peel potatoes, help fix the dinner, do the dishes and, at about 9 PM, start in on our homework. No time to rest from the time we got up in the morning until we were ready to drop. Never, ever, ever any time to play!

School was a three mile walk but we usually got a ride if it was raining. In the summer we had the additional task of picking apples off the ground and feeding them to the pigs.

In the morning my father would get up first and start the wood fire so that my mother could cook breakfast. On cold winter mornings we dressed in a hurry! There was one bedroom for the boys and one for the girls, my parents' room and a spare room. I had chores before school and took my turn milking the family cow. The lunch we took to school consisted of dry, unsliced bread (remember, no wax paper!) After school we'd reach our property gate and race down the driveway, pile into the pantry and bolt down what we could find. We were allowed anything except my mother's fancy cakes made for the Grange.

Before chores we'd change into other clothes because we girls had only one dress for school. If it was soiled, we washed it at night and ironed it in the morning.

My father was active in the community and helped other Portuguese get their immigration papers and other legalities in order; his kindness in this respect earned him many friends. The fact that we had the only telephone on the road helped as well and kept us in good touch with our neighbors.

In the '20s, the chickens got Newcastle disease, and my father juggled running a small grocery store and studying real estate. He frequently left his teenage children in charge until he noticed that we ate up all the candy and ice cream. My mother was very well read and the two of them joined every single service club there was. It was at this time that our social life improved somewhat. My father loved to go. He'd drop anything and say, "Let's go fishing!" My mother would jump at the chance. There were seven of us children and he'd take us on fishing trips and outings to the ocean, the Navarro River, the Russian River, the Estero. We were the only ones our age who knew how to swim.

In 1926, with a Sweet's Business School background, I went to work with my father in his real estate office. At one point I had helped him so much he gave me $500 and said I'd earned it. My sister and I used the money to cruise to Sitka and Whitehorse, Alaska. We had the time of our lives!

In the early '40s my husband, Desmond, and I purchased seven acres of the ranch and moved our own growing family to the homestead. Soon we found ourselves back in the poultry business during a very trying decade of war, much competition, and decreasing profits. In a moment of creative genius, my husband took our last dollars and invented an egg cleaner which was the very best of its kind. Unfortunately, the timing was poor. Lack of capital to mass produce and new egg-cleaning standards invoked by the Poultry Producers of Central California curbed Des' manufacturing venture. I was so depressed that I decided to visit a friend. She wanted to try selling some old things from her garage and I helped her write an ad for the newspaper. The yard sale was so successful that it inspired me to try a similar project. I, too, managed to sell everything. Taking my profits, my husband and I started purchasing furniture and antiques at auctions in San Francisco and, putting it on display in the empty chicken houses, we resold it to a post-war, furniture-needy public. Thus was born the family furniture business, currently owned by my son Paul and known as Praetzel's Fine Furniture.

Bertha Praetzel

EGG DAY 1922. LUTHER BURBANK, 73, ACCEPTS A CHICKEN HAT FROM MARJORIE PASKO. FROM LEFT: VIOLA BALDWIN, EDA PETERS, ZOUSA VALLIES, ALMA MOMSEN, WILMA ROACH. PHOTO COURTESY OF BEVERLY VLASTOS, DAUGHTER OF ALMA MOMSEN.

CANDLER AT FOURTEEN

My father died and we had to move to town. I went to work at the Poultry Producers, candling eggs, when I was 14. Our family doctor was on the Board of Education and he saw to it that I was excused from school. My sister Rose was already working there and she taught me candling.

You had four eggs, two in each hand and you rolled them before a light, looking for blood spots, broken shells (called blind checks, since they would only show before a light), and fifteen other categories, including reds, blues, greens and medium greens, cities (eggs with the air cell broken a little–they went to San Francisco for restaurants and bakeries), browns, peewees, jumbos, light dirties, medium dirties and extra dirties. The blues had lemon-colored yolks and were prized by the New York market.

We stood on concrete, surrounded by egg cases, and candled one lot at a time, that is, all the eggs brought in by a single rancher. We wrote out a tag for each lot indicating the number in each category by which the rancher was paid.

We recognized producers by their lots. "Mudballs" came from range birds in the wintertime. Fertile eggs had been produced for hatcheries but came to us as extras. The eggs from Rosenblum and Hayes were always clean and also from the Japanese. Germans, Danes and Swedes all had good eggs. Eggs that came from dairy ranches were not so clean; too little time to manage milking, keep the nests clean and clean the eggs. Dirty eggs went through the sanding machine or the washer.

Once a month each candler's work was checked for accuracy. About 200 candlers worked from 8 to 5 with a lunch break. At first I worked six days a week. Men had done the candling originally, but when they found out women were faster, men lost out. During the Depression, this meant that women had jobs and the men were at home to manage the poultry ranch.

After the 1929 Crash my wage was cut to 33.5 cents an hour. To keep the job I had to do 16 cases a day; anything over that paid five cents a case more. We worked like dogs for the extra five cents. Some days I could make four dollars.

Once I said to my supervisor, "I can work faster than the others and be done by three o'clock. May I go home then?"

His response was, "The cemetery is full of people like you." So we stayed on piece-work.

My sister, Rose Tiemann, entered in a competition on Egg Day in 1927 against other fast candlers. Rose really knew her eggs and won the title Champion Egg Candler of the World. For winning she received some money and a bouquet of paper roses each with a cottony baby chick in its center. After the pictures were taken, Rose had to give the bouquet back to the Chamber of Commerce. Later on, people in Europe who had seen her picture came to see her.

Hilda Tiemann Keehn   SEE ALSO PAGE 23

SPINNING THE CLUCKERS

My grandparents came from Denmark to Petaluma in 1903. They were Hans Hansen and Anna Marie Jorgensen.
As a child we worked with the chickens, checked on the baby chicks every night to make sure they weren't piling up or pecking each other. We smeared grey stuff under the wings of the adult birds to try to control lice.

My father called broody hens "cluckers." He'd put them in a cage suspended from the ceiling of the chicken house, and every time he went by he gave the cage a whirl. In two or three days they were through with clucking.

Once we worked almost all night moving birds to another chicken house. The sleeping hens were caught on the roost, placed in the coop, and carried to the roosts of their new home.

"Well," said my father, as we put the last chicken in the coop, "that's the last one. If we'd done her first, we'd've been finished long ago."

Towards the end of the laying season, the hens were caught and examined to determine if they were still laying. The system we used was devised by Walter Hogan who lived on Skillman Lane. He described it in *The Call of the Hen* published in 1913. If the poultryman could get three fingers between the pelvic bones, she was considered to still be a layer. Those who'd stopped laying were culled as non-producers and sold to the market for soup and fricassee.

If a chicken was diseased or dying my father picked it up by the head and swung it around with a jerk. Death was instantaneous. "Let the body do the work," he said.

We fought rats, weasels, and sparrows (which carried diseases), going from house to house with a dog and a BB gun. My father had an old mare that pulled the sled from door to door of the chicken houses. She would stop at each one, wait for us to load the sled with the buckets of eggs, then move at my father's command.

Before chick sexing was perfected we had an old brooder house that was used as a rooster house. When we bought chicks they'd be a mixture of pullets and cockerels. As the cockerels became recognizable (developed a comb), they were moved to the rooster house and were fed and fattened to go to the market at 11 or 12 weeks.

During the Depression, Mother went to work at the Poultry Producers packing plant, where the women candled eggs and were paid by the number of cases they packed. She told of one pretty woman who was favored by the manager, who saw to it that cases of clean eggs were brought for her to pack, while the rest of the women, including my mother, got cases with dirty eggs in them. When the plant workers unionized, the manager could no longer play favorites.

My folks eventually lost the place to G.P. McNear for a feed bill of $4,000. McNear had carried them for years.

Anna Hansen Harrigan
*and brother **Thurman Hansen***

WE ALWAYS HELPED EACH OTHER

All the ranches around Two Rock produced hatching eggs, not eggs for the table, but fertile eggs for the hatcheries. Since the birds were on free range and because of the wind and the fresh air, the hens were regarded as especially healthy, and therefore our eggs were in demand by the hatcheries.

I came here from Wisconsin in 1921 when I was 20. People used coal to heat brooder houses. You can still see the brick chimneys on some old buildings on Middle Two Rock Road.

In those days, the birds were kept in colony houses which were made to be movable. One time around 1922 or '23 my brother-in-law needed to move his birds and houses to a place across the county road, up the hill and over to the other side of the hill. There were about eight or ten colony houses and we built temporary floors into them. When the birds came in to roost at night we closed the door to keep them in. Then we hitched them by chains to the runners to a team of horses and pulled the colony houses with the birds inside to the new site over the hill. We moved one colony, eight or ten houses, a night.

I married Annie McCannon in 1927. We acquired this place and moved here in 1929. We planted the cypress trees to keep the wind off our living quarters. The redwoods came from Fort Bragg. A driver brought me little two inch trees in a package I could hold in my hand, in 1935. Now those redwoods are over 100 feet high.

After a while I built a brooder house, then colony houses. These colony houses were well built. Mine were 6 by 12

feet. Rough 1 x 10 redwood boards were cut five feet long
for the sides and the runners were 2 by 8s, 14 feet long, so
you could slope them. Each runner had a hole in the front to
put the chain through to move them. For the roof we used 1
x 4 tongue-and-groove redwood cut about four feet long.
We had 2 by 3s to support the 1 x 4s which were laid
vertically. It didn't matter if they leaked a little.

R oosts were the entire length, 2 by 2s, not nailed to the
side but held in slots. We turned them over each
month because they would start to bend in the middle from
the weight of the birds.

When I needed more colony houses, I'd get the lumber, cut
it to the proper lengths and pile it in my back yard. Neighbors, eight or ten of them, would come on a Sunday morning and we would make half a dozen or more houses in a
day. There'd be a big stew to eat. We never hired anyone.
We always helped each other.

We cooked feed for the chickens every day in big 20-gal-
lon boilers, built up on bricks, over a wood fire. We used
what was available—potatoes, herring, horse meat, soy
beans. In the morning we picked and chopped kale to add to
the mixture.

 Around Two Rock there were dairies and sheep but everyone also had a brooder house and chickens, perhaps only
1,000, but everyone had them. We all raised chickens to lay
eggs for the hatcheries out here on "the coast." I sold eggs to
and bought baby chicks from Hardin Hatchery and used
medicine from the Davis Chicken Pharmacy.

The hatcheries didn't like the idea of bigger chicken houses
or artificial lighting. They also specified that we would feed
the birds corn.

Boyd Roerden was working for McNear's when Hitler invaded Poland in 1939. He came out and said, "War started in Europe this morning. Wheat is going up. I can sell you wheat at $1.55 a hundred." The price was for carload lots at 20 tons to a car.

The war made a demand for meat birds A lot of people made money during the war raising broilers.

I started raising pullets, 10,000 every three months. I guess I raised millions. I retired in 1962.

Martin Mickelson

DRAGGING A COLONY HOUSE. *UNIV. OF MISSOURI AGRI. EXT. SVC. CIRC.* 453 (1942). COURTESY DR. FRANCINE A. BRADLEY, AVIAN SCIENCES, UC-DAVIS

YOU LEARNED

Holding two eggs in your left hand and a shoe-buffer covered with fine sandpaper in your right, you learned how to dry-clean eggs by turning them and sanding them lightly to remove only soiled bits. This method brought higher prices but at the cost of the outside edges of your left-hand fingernails.

By Marjorie Forster Sobel

PETE MATZEN WITH TRAYS OF INCUBATING EGGS AT PIONEER HATCHERY.
PHOTO BY RUSSELL LEE C. 1941. COURTESY OF THE LIBRARY OF CONGRESS.

FIFTY~SIX MILLION, ONE AT A TIME

My father came from Sweden a hundred years ago at the age of 19. He brought my mother, Edla, over in 1914 and they were married. He was a carpenter and was the contractor for Lowell High School in San Francisco.

In 1918, when I was three, we moved to Petaluma. My family went into the chicken business two years later. My father built a brooder house and three chicken houses, and carefully planted kale in straight rows. Like most Petaluma children, I worked with the chickens to help the family. When I graduated from high school in 1933, I was unable to find work because of the Depression.

We had heard in high school that the Japanese were able to "sex" [identify the gender of] newly hatched chicks with a good degree of accuracy. In the fall of 1934, my high school agriculture teacher, W. H. Van Dyke, told me that the hatcheries in Petaluma had started a chick sexing school. This fascinated me and I hurried to enroll.

Until the Japanese perfected the ability to ascertain gender, poultrymen were unable to distinguish between cockerels and pullets until the males developed combs at several weeks of age. Straight run chicks are roughly 50-50 male and female. The chicks were shipped to the buyers the day after hatching because they could survive the trip using the last of the nourishment already in their bodies. Farmers had to feed the entire flock until the cockerels could be culled.

As it is costly to raise birds you don't intend to keep, chick sexing made big changes in the economics of poultry raising as it now enabled farmers to raise all pullets from the very start, thus doubling the number of laying hens. Turkey raisers also benefited since the smaller hens were segregated from the heavier toms which would crowd them out.

Dr. Kiyoshi Masui first discovered the "eminence" (precursor of the genital organ) in male chickens in 1925. He learned by studying adult birds and then handling progressively younger males until he was able to discern the sex of day-old chicks. This fact was reported to the World Poultry Congress in 1927 in Ottawa, Canada. The Japanese soon organized a chick-sexing association and established an examination for licensing and, in 1932, decided to send sexors overseas.

In 1933 chick sexor Yogo gave a demonstration in British Columbia and again in Chicago. It caused a sensation. Hatchery men from Petaluma were impressed and arranged to have Yogo come to Petaluma, screen some chicks and prove the accuracy of chick sexing. The first school was in British Columbia in 1933 and the following fall, its graduates began teaching in Petaluma sponsored by the major hatcheries.

Classes met five days a week at the Must Hatch Hatchery, starting in September. Each hatchery had to furnish a weekly quota of day-old chicks for the students to study.

At first we watched our instructors and then gradually learned how to handle the chicks so as not to injure them, and then eventually to manipulate them so that one could invert the vent and determine whether it was male or female. We worked under intense lights, 200 and 300 watts. We were looking for the infinitesimal bud, the eminence, half the size of a pinhead.

It took three months of training full-time to attain the necessary expertise. Twenty-four students started the course and 15 passed the test in December. As this was the first chick sexing school in California and we were the first graduates, perfect accuracy wasn't required. Professor Bill Newlon from UC-Berkeley conducted the examination. Each student sexed 100 chicks, and then they were autopsied to verify results. One trainee had 100 percent accuracy and several 99 percent.

When we first started work for the hatcheries, we guaranteed 92 percent accuracy and they, in turn, guaranteed the buyer 90 percent. Soon the hatcheries raised the accuracy level to 95 percent and then to 98 percent. In later years a person's skill needed to be 99 percent accurate.

I taught myself how to sex turkeys, too, but it took a long time. First year I couldn't see any difference at all between a hen and a tom. Second year, I noticed a slight difference. Third year, I could sex turkeys. I sexed turkeys at Nicholas in Sonoma for 40 years.

Once I was called as a witness in Small Claims Court. A man who'd ordered cockerels was suing because he didn't get 10 percent pullets. His logic was, on pullet orders the guarantee was 90 percent accuracy so he assumed he should have received 10 percent pullets in his cockerel order. The judge ruled against him.

I was asked to teach chick sexing and I trained dozens starting in 1937.

Over the years I worked for a number of different hatcheries and had to keep a log in order to be paid properly. The basis was per chick. At first it was a half-cent a chick each;

at the end it was a little over two cents per chick.

In my 55 years I sexed more than 56 million chicks, the first for pay in December, 1934, and the final one at H&N Hatchery on March 19, 1989, one of the last chicks hatched in Petaluma.

I never dreamed I would outlast the hatcheries. I was one of the first chick sexors from the original group, the one who worked the longest, and the last one to quit.

Heimer C. Carlson

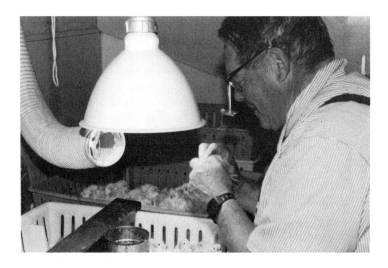

HISTORIC MOMENT, March 18, 1989. Heimer Carlson sexing his last box of White Leghorn chicks at H&N, the final hatch of the last hatchery in Petaluma. During his career, "Ham" appeared on the national television show, "Ripley's Believe It or Not!" Photo courtesy H.C. Carlson

THE CHICKEN PHARMACIST'S DAUGHTER

Anna Keyes Neilsen lived on Thompson Lane, three miles from town, with her younger sister Elizabeth and her father James E. Keyes from age five until she was a high school junior. The years spent on the ranch were approximately 1908 to 1919. Anna's mother died in 1910. Her father never remarried. Her father, who had been educated as a pharmacist, and had paid off the mortgage on the ranch, moved to town where he was a druggist for Joe Tuttle. He later began doing mail-order business dealing in medicines for chicken diseases. He established the Chicken Pharmacy on Main Street in 1923, took in Dr. Davis, a vet, as a partner and eventually sold out to him.

As a child, Anna's chores were many since her father had no help on the ranch. She worked by picking peas, planting kale, and helping to vaccinate the 11,000 laying hens, and was up at 5 AM to do some of her chores before school. Her comfort was a big swing in an oak tree. Her father did hire a housekeeper who cooked, cleaned, and sewed clothes for the girls, but Anna was not close to her. Mrs. Kennedy, who stayed for 18 years, "was bigoted and narrow-minded and hated educated people." But she did love Anna's younger sister "Bessie," and raised the girls.

"My father had been taught to compound medicines. Drug stores were changing, druggists were no longer compounding medicines, they were merely retailing medicines. Where he got the idea to establish a chicken pharmacy, I don't know. Yet he must have talked to poultrymen who came in to buy potassium to clean their water troughs of algae.

"I went to work for him there, filling capsules with compounds he had devised. I didn't work at the counter. There the poutrymen were asking for diagnoses.

"I do remember Hoganizing, a method of determining the best laying hens in a flock."

Anna Keyes Neilsen

INTERVIEW BY CHERYL JERN, SUMMARY BY MARILYN BRAGDON

AFRAID OF CHICKENS

My grandmother owned a chicken ranch. I was afraid of chickens after seeing their heads chopped off and the bodies run around the yard. Grandma eventually had to give up the business because she became attached to her chickens and wouldn't sell them.

Sometimes as children we'd raise chicks and consider them pets. When the truck came to take them to market we'd hide them or lie down in front of the truck to prevent it from driving away.

Petaluma's streets were cobbled then so horses wouldn't slip.

Some of my relatives were settlers of Penngrove; the Peters, Reiverts, Ronshiemers and Roaches lived in Petaluma.

Donna Griffith Adamson

MAX POEHLMANN

Pioneer Petaluma poultryman Max W. Poehlmann served in France during the first war. Afterwards he and his father opened a hatchery which operated until his retirement in 1970. Poehlmann died ten years later at age 90, a civic leader and sportsman, widely known throughout the county. —*ARGUS-COURIER* OBITUARY EXTRACT. PHOTO, 91

THE CAPTAIN'S GHOST

We had about six acres on I Street extension with three long chicken houses, a pullet house and a brooder house, together with a small cage operation. Maybe 10,000 chickens. We sold eggs to the Poultry Producers and fertilized eggs to the hatcheries.

My folks, Ted and Helen F. King, bought the ranch from the widow of a Captain Middleton, whose death over a chess board at a downtown club caused her to sell. The Captain's ghost haunted the place.

My jobs as a youngster were various through time: I was enlisted to carry feed to the chicken houses, gather eggs, feed and water the cockerels, help with vaccinations, pluck butchered chickens, haul dead chickens from the houses to the cans out in front where they were picked up by the tallow-works truck, care for some of the other animals (cow, calves, sheep, goat, pig, ducks, geese, rabbits), trap varmints, and scrape roosts. I wasn't really strong enough for this until about the time the business folded.

By *Thomas F. King*

SEE ALSO ACCOUNTS ON PAGES 47 AND 79.

FROM 4H TO PHD ~ DVM

My father's family was from Germany. They bought the ranch in 1900. Father lived into his 80s and Mother into her 90s. She was a Benedetti; they developed the Willie Bird Turkey. My brother, Ernie, stayed in the chicken industry on Western Avenue and another brother, Conrad, is in the hatchery business in Portland, as a broker of exotic birds.

As a child, my daily schedule was: up at 6:30, milk two or three cows; mix the chicken feed (kale, barley and meat scraps), place in cooker and then crumble the mash into 20 buckets. 7 AM: climb on the horse-drawn wagon/sled, dispense the feed into the troughs of seven chicken houses. Next, run the milk through the separator, eat breakfast and walk to school.

I was active in 4H; my junior year high school project was to build a brooder house in which to raise 500 pullets. I could raise three batches a year since it took four months for each batch. I made between $300 and $500 per batch. My uncle went on vacation during my senior year. I used his ranch to put in chickens and made $2000 for college. I supported myself as a lab tech at $50 a month, took a BA, MA and a PhD at Berkeley. I was a microbiologist and than studied to be a veterinarian. Eventually I became the chairman of the department in chicken disease research and directed the efforts to create a vaccine effective against Marek's Disease, a fatal disease that affects the lymph cells of chickens.

It took 25 years to develop the vaccine. His distinguished academic career brought him 22 awards and honors.

Ben Burmester   AS TOLD TO MARILYN BRAGDON

CULL HENS AND CRACKED EGGS

I was expected to collect and clean eggs every afternoon after school, help herd baby chicks under the brooder in the evening, and toss young hens up on the roost after dark, to keep them from smothering themselves in heaps in the corners. After full dark, we took our dogs and made rat raids on all the chicken houses. What rats the dogs didn't catch, we'd bash with clubs.

Life on our chicken ranch was a miserable experience for me.

I was the oldest of four children, a teenager, and had enjoyed life in San Francisco and Marin County during my father's Navy years. Ranch life in Petaluma was a far cry from that!

At this time it was hard for family operations to survive; we ate a *lot* of cull hens and cracked eggs. There was very little time or money for extracurricular activities, and weekends meant herding and culling or vaccinating chickens. Hard work and heavy lifting took their toll on my parents and they had health problems as a result. For me, the happiest day of my life came when the doctor diagnosed my respiratory problems as an allergy to feathers.

Chicken ranch life made me and my sister and brothers stronger and more cohesive than we might have been otherwise, but in every other way it was a period of my life about which I have very few rosy memories.

By *Prue King Draper*

SEE ALSO ACCOUNTS ON PAGES 45 AND 79.

THE PRINCE WHO WAS
A CHICKEN FARMER

He was ten when the Bolsheviks came to power. The grandson of Czar Alexander III and Empress Marie Fedorovna, Prince Vasili Romanov was born in a thousand-room palace into the family which had ruled Russia from 1613 to 1917. He grew up to raise chickens in Sonoma County.

His father, Grand Duke Alexander, was the czar's cousin and founder of the royal air force, and his wife was Grand Duchess Xenia, Nicholas' sister. The kings of England, Greece and Denmark were his great-uncles.

Prince Vasili and his family were rescued by a British battleship sent by their cousin, King George V, at the time of the assassinations of the czar, the czarina and their children. Although he had the means, he never returned to Russia, but was reportedly optimistic that the reforms of Mikhail Gorbachev would mean freedom for his countrymen.

His first job was as a cabin boy and in later years he was a shipyard worker and a stockbroker in San Francisco and a winemaker in the Almaden Valley.

He told an interviewer, "In my colorful career, I think I enjoyed the chicken farm most." It was reportedly in Glen Ellen for several years during WWII. Raising the birds was his "part of the war effort." He died two weeks shy of 82.

San Francisco Chronicle, June 28, 1989, obituary extract

BABY CHICKS IN MY HAND

In the hatcheries—almost all of them in downtown Petaluma—the eggs were placed in huge incubators and individual eggs were turned over with a rocker motion, in imitation of the setting hen. Twenty-one days later, the chicks pecked their way out of the eggs and within the day were sexed. The cockerels were generally destroyed and the rest packed for shipping in ventilated shipping boxes made of cardboard and wooden slats.

At the ranch, the chicks were received at the brooder house, close to the farm dwelling and smaller than the big chicken houses. Often the responsibility of the farm wife, baby chicks had to be watched closely. They were kept warm by the hundreds under a big sheet-metal dome that trapped warm air from a kerosene or gas-fired stove.

My father, Max Kortum, had come to Petaluma in 1922 as a Poultry Husbandry graduate of UC-Davis employed by Sperry Flour Company, a large supplier of grain to G.P. McNear, a local feed miller for the area's ranchers. My father visited the poultrymen to talk about feeds and feeding, the need for ventilation in the chicken houses, diseases and inoculations, etc. He introduced the idea of the balanced formula in the mash and it changed the way chickens were fed in Petaluma.

Starting in 1928, he was owner or part owner of four hatcheries himself, the last one on Ely Road where I still live in the farmhouse built in 1915.

As a child, I went with him to deliver baby chicks just hours old from our hatchery on North Main Street. We would unload the boxes, each holding 100 chicks, at the brooder house. We picked up several baby chicks at a time from the compartments of the shipping box and, kneeling, placed them inside a foot-high fence on clean straw at the outskirts of the brooder. The chicks ran toward the warmth and went to sleep there, standing up. I can remember how it felt to have the baby chicks in my hand, three or four of them at a time, their bodies resting on my fingers and their legs between my fingers. I remember the warm smell of the chicks and the clean smell of the straw. The babies would be kept there until they feathered out and were ready for the weather outside.

I remember a delivery in the first heat of summer to Sonoma Valley. We stopped in the shade of a big walnut tree on Lakeville Highway to cool the chicks, some of which were dying. We pulled the tops from the ventilated boxes and waited there for the fresh air to revive and save the surviving chicks.

The birds lived, several hundred at once, in chicken houses, roosting at night on sloping wire and slat constructions, built above the floor. During the day the hens were allowed into large wire pens, and they could return inside the chicken house to lay eggs in box nests attached to the walls. Chicken houses on my father's place had a yard on each side. One was accessible to the chickens, the other was planted to kale. Every day we would pull kale leaves off the plants to throw to the chickens and when this great cabbage plant reached maturity, the chickens were turned into the yard to clean up the last of the leaves from the old plants. This left stalks as big around as my arm, leaning at all angles. Then the first yard was sealed off from the birds, plowed under and planted to new young kale plants.

Another type of housing was the colony house, which held perhaps 40 birds. They were built on skids and had no floors. They could be pulled by horses to new locations on the big ranches. They were of two sizes; a smaller one for roosting at night, and the other for laying. The young hens, seven to nine-month-old pullets, were moved to the colony houses as they started to lay eggs. These little houses dotted the hills for years, long after it became more economical to keep large flocks of hens in long chicken houses with enclosed yards.

When it was necessary to catch birds to doctor or move them, we used a coop. This is a wire and slat crate with two compartments and sliding doors on the top. Coops were used to ship live adult chickens to market and to move birds to new locations on the ranch. A different kind of coop was also used to trap birds driven from the chicken house into the waiting cage. From this coop the hen could be examined to see if she were still laying or could be treated for disease, and then set free in the yard.

My mother cleaned the eggs with sandpaper. The air of the egg room was filled with dust from the shells and chicken droppings that had dried on the egg. Some eggs needed to be soaked and washed by hand. Then the eggs were packed in cartons and the cartons in cases, to be taken twice a week to the Poultry Producers, a big plant on the Petaluma River, downtown. She wore a homemade print cotton house-dress and listened to the soap operas on the radio each afternoon as she worked. "Better," she said, "than going over my own worries."

Hens lay one egg a day and average five a week. My job sometimes as a youngster was to gather eggs; but a scary part was to encounter a broody hen, one that has decided to try to hatch several eggs already in a nest and acts menacing as she fiercely defends her clutch against invaders. With her head lowered and beak open, warning me with a hissing sound, she made herself larger by raising her feathers. She defeated me. We kept White Leghorns, a breed chosen for their almost year-round laying capacity. The roosters were known for their willingness to attack and fight. Our ranch didn't always keep roosters in the flocks. They are usually maintained on ranches where the hens must produce fertile eggs for the hatcheries.

Cleaning the chicken houses was physically hard work and fell ordinarily to my brothers, our cousin Jack Hoeck, and our friend Jack Eatherton. Chicken manure collected under the roosts, had to be scraped up with hoes and rake and shovel, and then removed by wheelbarrow. My father paid Jack Eatherton one dollar a day, raised to $1.50 when it was time for junior college.

Another working member of the ranch was our rat terrier Boleybop, who accompanied the workers wherever they went. Rats were a serious problem to the poultrymen. They not only carried disease but chewed holes in the sacks, ate the grain and caused enormous waste.

These short-haired terriers were bred to catch rats by the Markuson family in Penngrove.

On the trail of a rat they barked sharply, then crawled fearlessly under the chicken houses or ran still barking into the corners of the feed room; then, facing the rat head on, would grab and shake it in one incredibly fast snapping movement, breaking its back.

Maxine Kortum Durney   PHOTOGRAPHS ON PAGE 63

FLATTOP, CABINET OR WALK~IN

My father, William Henry Bihn, moved to California from Ohio in 1903. With the help of a loan from George P. McNear, a Petaluma feed and grain merchant, he and his brother Sylvan started a hatchery. His wife Anna Rose subsequently joined him in the business.

The hatchery was a wooden frame building just outside the city limits on Bodega Avenue. The first incubators, called "flattops," were built on the premises. Each unit held only one tray of eggs. It was warmed by a pipe full of water heated by natural gas and circulated by convection. A thermometer was just above the tops of the eggs and the operators tried to keep the temperature at 103 degrees (which meant the interior of the egg was about 99 degrees) by opening and closing a vent. Humidity was not controlled but they still had a high hatchability.

Bihn bought fertile White Leghorn hatching eggs from independent famers under contract to him, paying 10 cents a dozen above the fresh egg market quotation. On the fourth day of incubation, the eggs were candled and those which were infertile (showed no sign of a developing embryo) were sold at a lower grade, often to bakeries.

As business expanded, the trays—four to an incubator unit— were made in such a way that the eggs rested on beveled, half-inch redwood slats. Twice a day the eggs had to be turned by hand to prevent the chick embryo from sticking in one spot inside the egg. A worker would pull out a tray, give it a little tilt and all the eggs would flop to the left. The next time they pulled out the trays they'd give them another little tilt and the eggs would flop to the right.

This was done from day one until hatching at 21 days. The baby chicks were delivered by horse and wagon. Often Anna Rose would make the delivery, 100 chicks packed in each crate made of box-wood with straw in the bottom.

Petaluma shipped enormous numbers of chicks by rail to poultry farms in Utah, Colorado and Idaho. The baby chicks could survive a three-day journey in the heated and air-conditioned cars. The farmers in those three states considered Petaluma chicks to be the best obtainable in the '20s and '30s.

Male White Leghorn chicks (cockerels) were not of economic value, only pullets (females) were, and they were raised solely to lay eggs. Some cockerels were fed for a few months and then sold as broilers. The term "spring chicken" comes from the fact that about 99 percent of chickens hatch in February, March and April. When day-old chick sexing was perfected in the late '30s, cockerels weren't particularly marketable because the heavier meat breeds were better for eating so the males were destroyed at the time of sexing. But before long, cockerel chicks were sold to mink breeders who needed protein to supplement feed so the mink could reproduce.

William A. Bihn

WE FOUND ARROWHEADS THERE

My grandfather, Elisha Light, was a gold miner, an hotel operator and a dairyman. I was born on his 320-acre ranch in Chileno Valley. With his beard and his hat, he looked Amish.

My other grandfather, Henry Schlake, brought his family here from Germany, lived at the Burdell Ranch, and later ranched, starting in the 1880s, near where Petaluma Airport is now, raising hay, grain, cows and chickens. They sold eggs locally and sometimes shipped them to San Francisco. Their daughter, my mother, married Elisha Hector Light.

I lived on the Chileno Valley ranch until I was five, when my father purchased 40 acres on Ely Road, and raised hay, cows and about 500 chickens. This was before the turn of the century. We lived in a two room house which my father built. He died in 1902, when I was nine or ten. Then my uncle came and we expanded it for him. Later, about 1910, my mother added three bedrooms, a bath and a living room.

The first thing my father planted was a family orchard, mostly apples. One was called a "lemon apple," and ladies in town waited for those apples to ripen. They made a lovely lemon-tasting white applesauce.

When my sister and I came home from school there was sometimes time to play, but there was also work—gathering eggs, tending to the chickens. But I never learned to milk. My mother had milked a string of 20 cows when she was young. She didn't want me to learn to milk.

She had an incubator, a Must Hatch, made by the elder Mr. Bourke. Later she had a Jubilee Incubator. My mother hatched eggs for other people as well as for us. There were three or four trays, probably two or three hundred eggs at a time, heated by a kerosene burner, at the side of the incubator. Water, just a small amount, had to be kept in the incubator to keep the moisture up. You'd go out once a day to trim the wick, to keep the heat up. Eggs had to be turned by hand. This was in the early 1900s.

I went to work for Petaluma Incubator Company, across from Hill Plaza Park, in 1910 or 1911, typing and doing secretarial work for Lyman Byce, his son Malcolm and other members of the firm. Byce did a worldwide business as the largest manufacturer in the world of incubators and brooders. Both were heated with kerosene, later with electricity. Some were large enough to hold thousands of eggs.

World War I put Byce's out of business. Petaluma Incubator Company's shipments were in danger of being torpedoed. Byce had been shipping goods and equipment and even "Dr. Hess's" medical supplies. I worked for Byce for four years before I married Edwin Kelsey.

My in-laws settled here on Old Adobe Road in the 1860s and purchased several large tracts of land on the east side. Their holdings eventually came to us. On our property down at the creek behind us is a sheltered area with a good spring and the dark earth indicating it was used by Indians. We found arrowheads there.

Emily Light Kelsey

IN THE DARK THE COUNTRYSIDE LOOKED LIKE A CITY

I am the daughter of Frank and Martha Roderick. Our family raised chickens from 1917 to 1935, the year I graduated from Petaluma High School. On our ten acres on Magnolia Avenue we kept about 5,000 laying hens in three large houses with outdoor runs.

My brother Wayne—five years younger—and I had farm chores such as looking after the baby chicks. My dad would buy an assortment of day-old chicks from a Petaluma hatchery and prepare the brooder house by cleaning, spraying with disinfectant and putting new straw on the floor. We'd have the brooder stove going full blast when the babies came, packed in their cardboard boxes. We'd lift them out carefully and put them around the brooder on the fresh straw.

During the day the baby chicks ate mash and chick feed. After they were two or three weeks old they were allowed to run around their own little yard during the day until it was time for us kids to chase them back in their house at nightfall.

When the birds reached ten weeks old, my brother and I helped with the long, hot job of separating the pullets from the cockerels. Our birds were graded, vaccinated and moved to a larger house. Chickens were moved in coops: wooden-framed, wire-sided boxes, each with two compartments. Each side could hold 12 hens or 20 fryers.

We kept the pullets to raise for egg production and sold the rest to the market for meat birds, fryers.

The young pullets would lay peewees, eggs too small for the market but fine for household cooking. We culled older hens from the flock and sold them for stewing. Meanwhile the young pullets matured and began to lay full-size eggs.

When the Cotati Speedway was torn down, my dad bought some salvaged lumber and built houses for the chickens. Water troughs were hung outside the hen houses and medication was put in the water. The hens put their heads through a long slit in the side wall to drink. We purchased vaccines and medicines to combat coccidiosis and Newcastle disease at the Chicken Pharmacy on Main Street. We also bought colored celluloid rings for leg bands.

Ranchers fed chickens a variety of grains, but I remember my father's mixture was wheat, barley and milo maize. He'd empty sacks of these grains into a big bin and mix it with a short-handled scoop shovel. We saved the empty burlap sacks and sold them to a dealer.

All the poultry raisers were plagued with rats attracted by the grain. No matter how hard a rancher tried to combat them, rats still infested the countryside. My brother and I loved to hunt them. We'd say, "Let's go get rats!" Our ranch dogs, Spot, a stout fox terrier, and Maggie, a bird dog with large paws and an unknown pedigree, would tear off towards the nearest hen house.

Dad stored extra troughs under the high end of the hen houses. Rats burrowed under them, so we'd pull the boards away and let the dogs go at it. First Maggie with her big paws would dig into a rat hole and then she'd let Spot sniff down it. If they weren't close enough to the rat, Maggie would take over again and dig the hole deeper. Spot would stand by quivering for the kill. When we had rounded up enough for one day, Maggie would put all the dead rats in a pile with their heads pointing the same direction, and dad would shovel them up.

Chickens' greens were kale or a low vine called rape which was cut with a scythe. I can still see my father in the kale patch. He'd pick a kale leaf and tuck it under his arm until he collected a bunch. Then he'd put the bunch in a burlap bag he dragged along tied to his waist. Then he chopped up the leaves with the kale cutter in the barn. The chickens also ate oyster shells mixed in with the mash. Barges brought shell up the Petaluma River to the mills to be ground up as a supplement to strengthen eggshells.

In the dark the countryside looked like a city with all the lighted hen houses. The idea was to give the hens a longer day so they'd lay more eggs. Dad rigged his own timer by welding a lever on the back of an old alarm clock to trip the switch and turn on the lights while he was still comfortable in bed. It seems as though the chicken ranches were all north and west of Petaluma.

We all pitched in with chores every afternoon at 3:30. Dad would hitch the farm horse to a wagon filled with grain to feed the chickens. Everyone in the family would have a large bucket to gather eggs from the nests. We put the full buckets in the wagon to be hauled back to the egg house. In later years we had a more modern Model T flatbed truck.

The next day we graded and cleaned the eggs, which had remained cool overnight in the egg house with its dirt floor. If we were in doubt about the size of the egg, we'd put it on a little tin scale. If the pointer went down, we knew the egg was of regular size, but if the pointer stayed upright, we knew the egg was undersized. We'd have two cases going at a time; one for regulars and one for undersized.

We packed the eggs in wooden cases, each holding ten layers of three dozen each for a total 30 dozen eggs. Dad sold the eggs to a dealer who came to the ranch three times a week to collect the eggs. We sold the chicken manure to farmers for fertilizer.

Besides chickens, dad raised pigs, rabbits, turkey and ducks to sell and to eat. We did our own butchering. We'd buy a half a side of beef and keep it in our rented cold storage locker.

Dad always milked three cows. He'd put the milk through the separator and feed the skimmed milk to the hogs and he'd sell the cream. We kept enough whole milk for our household use, the cream for our homemade butter and whipped cream and for coffee.The rest of the milk was poured into a pitcher for drinking and cooking.

We raised our own vegetables, fruit and berries. I can still remember picking heaps of string beans and digging up potatoes. We picked fresh tomatoes right off the vines at meal time. My mom would can pears, peaches and apricots and make jelly from berries. We picked our cherries and apples from farmers' orchards.

We bought sugar and flour in hundred-pound sacks and emptied them into kitchen bins. The empty cotton bags were washed, bleached and hemmed for dish towels. With the flour and our own lard (fat rendered from butchering a pig) we made pies. We cooked on a wood stove with an oven in the winter and a large propane hot plate in the summer.

We had a well and a tank with a gravity feed system for our water supply. I remember that the pump was always going out—a broken belt, a burnt-out motor.

Our telephone was on a party line with ten other families. We always knew when somebody got a call: all eleven phones would ring. One neighbor had two short rings plus one long. Our number was 44F4: four rings on the 44F line.

Our car was a 1922 Reo open touring car with side curtains over the isinglass windows. It took over two hours to drive from Petaluma to Sausalito over the old Corte Madera grade, and 23 minutes on the ferry to the City.

On summer Sundays, we'd go to the beach. A crowd of relatives and friends would have a potluck dinner at noon. Chickens were fed a little later on those days. Since chicken ranching usually kept us close to home, we had lots of company on holidays and Sundays. We always had relatives for holiday dinners.

Sometimes we would buy a block of ice in Petaluma and chop it up to use in a wooden freezer and make ice cream. We'd also buy a watermelon and put it on ice.

For entertainment we listened to the radio, read the Sunday newspaper and went on picnics. We'd go swimming at Boyes Hot Springs, driving by the flat hay fields east of Petaluma where it's all houses now.

Lavelle Marie Roderick Donovan

H.A. WEINLAND OF SONOMA FARM BUREAU AT THE PETALUMA EGG LAYING CONTEST. COURTESY DR. FRANCINE A. BRADLEY, AVIAN SCIENCES, UC-DAVIS.

MY BEST YEAR

I was born July 24, 1890. I got through the third grade and then I had to go to work. I was a farmer and I didn't have time to go to school.

I'm from Italy; there's no industry, just farmers in Cordenones. I was married for about a week, left my wife with the family and went to Canada. Looking for work, I went to Oregon, then California.

I worked in a cement factory, a cannery, at a shipyard in San Francisco and washed dishes at the St. Francis Hotel. I saved for two years to bring my wife over from Italy.

Then we came up to Santa Rosa after the First War. I heard about the chickens in Petaluma. First I rented a small place, then I decided to buy the land here on Todd Road. It cost me $200 an acre. Then we started to build, the house and chicken houses.

First I built the brooder house. Then I built a 20 by 40 foot chicken house. The next year another 40 foot, then another 40 foot. I had about 1,400 White Leghorns and some Rhode Island Reds. I used to go with horse and wagon and take the eggs to the Sebastopol plant.

My wife took care of the baby chicks and cleaned and packed the eggs, about 30 dozen in a box. Eggs brought 12 cents a dozen during the Depression. At least we did all our own work; when they couldn't pay the help, a lot of chicken men went broke, but I didn't have to pay nobody. Those were tough years. We never went around with the car burning gas for fun, never went to the movies, all those years. We used to kill the pig and make our own salami. We had the experience from the old country.

My best year in the business? When I went out of the business! Now the money's gone, the eggs are gone, the health is gone, the times are gone. I've been pretty lucky, never heavy sickness. After thirty years in the chicken business? My advice is be patient and not to look for too much.

David Marson *as told to his grandchildren*
Richard Marson and Renée Vences de Marson

[David Marson died shortly before his 100th birthday.–Ed.]

JACK HOECK CLEANS EGGS ON THE MAX KORTUM PLACE IN 1940.
ACCOUNT ON PAGE 52. PHOTO BY KARL KORTUM.

THE KORTUM FAMILY RAT TERRIER, BOLEYBOP, WITH A HARVEST
OF RATS FROM THE FEED ROOM. PHOTO BY KARL KORTUM.

THIRTY~NINE YEARS
WITH THE POULTRY PRODUCERS

My parents, John and Emma Johnson, came from Sweden to Petaluma with 75 cents between them. My dad was a charter member of the Poultry Producers. He died when I was twelve. I learned to candle eggs in 1935, at Nye and Nissen, and I wasn't paid for learning. I went to work in 1937 for the Poultry Producers and candled there until 1944 when I went to work in the office, adding up the tags. Later I was in sales, making out the invoices for the trucks. I'd call and get orders—San Francisco, Marin, Concord, Fort Bragg, Willits, Santa Rosa. The head office would decide on the price for the day. Or we would give a store a break if they bought in volume or if they were going to advertise.

We also handled sales of meat birds. Farmers would bring in their live, culled hens; the birds were hung on a conveyor belt, their throats were cut, they bled, and then the pickers removed their feathers. This was called "New York dress."

The move to San Leandro came in 1957. Automation was involved, but it wasn't foolproof. Checked eggs, eggs with broken shells, got in with the good eggs. Our product was no longer perfect.

I continued to work for Poultry Producers until the plant closed. My 39 years with them made me the second longest employee.

Alta Johnson Mariola

BROODERS BY THE BOXCAR

Park Van Bebber, Herbert Sweed, and my father, Ernest, began Rex Mercantile in Petaluma in 1907, the year I was born. They featured hardware supplies for poultry producers and planned to add groceries, feed and dry goods later.

My father came from Kansas. He hopped a freight train and rode out here with the hobos to visit his uncle, who got him a job with Ludwig Schluckebier, a poultryman.

My mother was a Lohrman, the daughter of a German father and a Danish mother. Her family operated a chicken ranch on Lohrman Lane. For a while they grew cabbage and cucumbers and made sauerkraut and dill pickles which they sold by the barrel in San Francisco. My grandparents would put lighted candles on a pine tree at Christmas which brought visitors to see the "crazy German" custom.

When I was old enough my father wanted me to learn all the phases of the hardware store operation. I swept the floor. I was a plumbing apprentice for awhile and a book-keeper for a year. When I was nineteen, my brother and I began to take over the business because my father wasn't well. Our store catered to poultrymen; Tomasini's Hardware took care of the needs of dairymen, mostly Italian.

We bought poultry fencing, pipe and brooders by the railway boxcar. We sold egg buckets, egg scales and, later on, automatic valves for poultry watering systems. Wholesale salesmen called on us every week; we had sales reps go out to the chicken ranches which were to the north and northwest of town.

Saturdays were busy for us. The farmers came to town to sell eggs, buy feed, fencing, nails, pipe and fittings. They hitched their horses at the plaza. Since every farm needed a well and a water system, we started a well-drilling business and a plumbing business. We sold builders' hardware, kitchen goods and Bavarian china from Europe.

We had hundreds of charge accounts of owners of small farms, 10 acres or so. Things started to go downhill even before the '30s. Farmers who had always paid once a month learned they could get better prices for their eggs in the fall. When egg sales were slow, they said, "Mr. Hobbie, we can't pay you this month." They asked to be carried until fall when prices would be better.

I remember how elated farmers were in 1931 when the price paid for a dozen eggs went from 18 to 21 cents. We extended credit to thousands of them in the mid-'30s but we had to borrow from the bank to do it. Then the ranchers would come in the fall and say, "We can't pay." Wholesalers refused to carry us. We sent out collectors – Sherman Boivin was one – who'd say, "You owe us $500. How about $10?"

While we had hundreds of dollars out on a farmer, feed dealers had thousands. They were smarter; they sought protection and took mortgages on the ranches. We didn't. We had many ranchers who went through bankruptcy and we lost thousands of dollars. I saw that the other firms in town had the same problem, but Tomasini did not hit bottom as we did.

One day my father said the banker Al Behrens wanted us to come in to see him. He told us, "I have orders to collect, but if you will not borrow more, but pay 1 percent each month, I'll carry you."

Then came the real Depression. Things were going badly; we had to cut our help in half. We said to the employees, "You can leave or work half-time for half the salary." They all stayed on and worked full-time at half pay. Our extreme times lasted about six months, but it took 10 years to pay off our debt to the bank.

Our store burned down in 1942, leaving a four foot thick pile of ashes. Our old friend Schluckebier called and said, "You can take over our business. You can have it today and pay it off later as you can." We said No. I'll never forget that phone call.

We started all over again. In the 1940s prices began to go up once more and we built up our business again. Some of the ranchers even paid off.

George Hobbie

DEBEAKING

We would debeak them when they were two or three weeks old. This was to keep them from injuring each other by pecking out their eyes. Chickens gang up on each other and kill.

We used a little electric hotplate and ran the beak down over it to take off the sharp point but always left enough beak for the bird to be able to pick up feed and drink.

Our Sunday meal was always chicken; sometimes chicken and dumplings, sometimes fried chicken, sometimes roast chicken. My father killed the birds, my mother defeathered them and I cleaned them. I loved to do it, to see the insides, all those little eggs, it was interesting to me.

Jan Day Thompson

Daughter of Ralph and Alexis Day [who died in 1990 at age 82].

CAT CEMETERY

I grew up on a chicken ranch on Gossage Avenue where the sandy, clayey soil of the garden and chicken pens was riddled with gopher runs. Cats abounded; they were important, especially good rat catching cats, and they helped keep down gophers and mice. When distemper struck the cats, we held funerals for them, burying them in cemeteries of our own devising, suiting the cat's religion. Like Cypress Hill Cemetery in Petaluma, there was a burial place for Catholic cats, Protestant cats and Jewish cats.

A man came every afternoon from his plant in the Liberty District with chopped meat for my father to give to the chickens. The meat was in a square can, I remember, with the lid cut out. It was horse meat. The children were afraid of him and ran away when he came. He was the one who came for our old horse when it couldn't get up from the ground anymore.

Many who came to Petaluma to become chicken farmers had no knowledge of how to raise birds. My father and many other poultrymen depended on the Farm Advisor. He was Frank Mugglestone from the University of California, and he had an office in Petaluma.

Vanette Ott Bunyan

BAREFOOT IN THE MASH

O ur ten acre chicken ranch was on Gravenstein
Highway in Cotati. My parents were Samuel and
Althea Focht, and we had two long rows of chick-
en houses, a granary, and two brooder houses. We collected
the eggs in buckets two or three times a day and then would
clean them at a contraption my father devised: we held
dirty eggs against an electrically driven emery belt. We
washed very dirty eggs and used cracked eggs in our
kitchen. We ate lots of angel food and sponge cakes.

My father took the eggs in a horse-drawn wagon to the
Poultry Producers plant in Cotati three times a week after
we had packed them in crates. He brought home empty
crates and sacks of mash and grain. I remember thinking
we had gone up in the world when we discontinued using
the horse and wagon and got a Model A sedan which my
father built into a truck to do his delivery.

Once a month he would clean out the litter in the henhouse,
which would take a day of hard work for both my parents.
He'd clean the droppings from the roosts weekly, and still
used the horse and wagon for this.

We had to cull out the nonproducers and sell them, vaccinate the pullets, and put ointment on the baby chicks who'd
peck each other. All this required catching chickens and
putting them into coops. We children weren't too unhappy
when we escaped any of these jobs by being in school or
having other, easier things to do.

My father mixed his own mash out of a variety of ground
up grains. When I was a very little girl, I used to climb up
on a pile of the mash and kick it around with my bare feet.

My father didn't protest and now I wonder why. He fed this mash, milo or grain to the chickens and they had free access to oyster shells. We also grew and fed them kale.

Later, when we were older and came home for vacations, it was nice to know that things hadn't changed and there were still eggs to gather and pack.

Martha Focht Wohletz

BLOOD TESTING

I worked in a crew for Poehlmann Hatchery checking chickens in health screening. A crew of six or seven of us went out before dawn to the breeding farms that supplied eggs to the hatchery and rounded up chickens from the roosts. Hens and roosters all had to be blood-tested for the disease which affected chicks. It was dusty, dirty work to catch and cage the birds, and roosters would often attack with their long, sharp spurs.

Each hen was first checked to see if she was still in production, and culled if she were through laying. Then a worker pulled out a feather or two from the wing joint. This produced a drop of blood which was tested by another worker with a reagent, and the results were recorded. For this I was paid 75 cents an hour, pretty good pay at that time. Once, my mother woke me after I'd taken a long turn at work at pulling feathers because I was plucking wool from her good blanket and had pulled out almost a square foot of it.

I can't remember ever catching a chicken that did have the disease.

Bob Stimson   PHOTO ON PAGE 80

OF COURSE WE TALKED

My mother, Nellie, the daughter of a Scottish sea captain named Swain, was born in the Hawaiian Islands. My father, Manuel Figueira, was from the Azores and came to work on the sugarcane plantations. We kept chickens, I remember, and we sold extra eggs to an old Chinese man who went door to door buying an egg here and an egg there.

As children we spoke Portuguese, English and a little Hawaiian. My father came to Oakland to be treated by a Chinese herb doctor. My family liked California and stayed on. My father went to work for the Northwestern Pacific Railroad. This was in 1923.

I was scared to go to school where boys and girls would be together—in the islands, we had separate schools. We had been bilingual, but I remember when I asked my uncle what time school was out in the afternoon in Petaluma, I used the Hawaiian word "pau." He said I should no longer use those words.

I went to work for the Poultry Producers in December, 1926, just before my 16th birthday. If you lived in town, as we did, you had to go to school one afternoon a week if you were under 18. How we studied at that special school! Eventually we took a test to graduate.

Those were good days at the Poultry Producers, with about 50 candlers when I started, three alleys of candlers. Later there were more. We had a good time: picnics, barbecues, hay rides. We used to hike up Sonoma Mountain.

Someone would get married; we'd all chip in money for a present. The company would have a big dance in San

Francisco and we would all dress up in long dresses. Top of the Fairmont, once; later, Lido's in North Beach.

Our supervisor was Fred Boysen, called "Pop." Every week he lectured us, a real sad tale and we believed him. "The inspector was here and he found dirty eggs. Be sure you do your work right. Stop talking when you're working." Of course we talked, it got boring just standing there.

Walter Rasmussen came and played the piano during our lunch hour and we all danced. It was fun working there. In the beginning there was no heat except what came from a pot-bellied stove. They had black curtains around our stations to darken our cubicles and they helped keep the drafts off.

We worked at night during the spring, going back to work after supper; lots of eggs to do in the spring. During the War we worked a regular nine-hour day.

I quit when I got married in 1935, but after the baby was born, I'd leave the baby with my mother and go back and visit every day for coffee break. Pop Boysen said, "You might as well come back to work. We need you." I was there until the plant closed in 1957.

Anne Figueira Peterson

A KALE PATCH. COURTESY DR. FRANCINE A. BRADLEY, AVIAN SCIENCES, UC-DAVIS

THE WOMEN WOULD BE CRYING

My father came from the Isle of Föhr. He had a chicken ranch on Bodega Avenue. My mother's family was also from Föhr, originally a German holding. My grandfather, Martin Bundesen, was a ship's captain who became a rancher. He helped found the Mercantile Exchange, an egg co-op, which evolved into the Poultry Producers of Central California.

I was born in 1911. My two sisters and my brother and I all attended Wilson School. We came home every afternoon to work. We had 37 acres with all the birds in colony houses. At one time my father sold large eggs for a dollar a dozen, shipped to San Francisco on the steamer *Gold*. He went broke in the '30s and was taken over by the feed company, Golden Eagle.

My parents separated and I left home when I was seven. I went to live with and work for Jack Hoover, a poultry dealer. I'd have to catch chickens in the morning before school and often I'd miss the first hours. A year later Hoover was caught with phony weights. I left to live with my sister and her husband.

Chickens used to be shipped on the steamers but trucks came to replace them. Soon all the produce was put on trucks—eggs, chickens, potatoes. I drove my truck to the City starting when I was 16. It was a Model T Ford with the famous insufficient gear ratio and also bum brakes. Over the Corte Madera grade I'd have to shift down to control it.

I would have a load of 25 coops holding live birds, either 25 stewing hens per coop or 50 broilers (young roosters). Everyone would get off the road when I came, the road was so narrow. It took two hours from Petaluma to the Sausalito ferry.

In 1929 I began to buy and sell chickens. I was 18. I paid cash on the spot. In those days a farmer might have a whole chicken house full of birds he wanted to sell so he could move in his new pullets. They'd be three, four or five years old, all mixed together. Chickens went to commission houses, mostly on Battery and Front streets in San Francisco, where they were fed for a week on a milk mash to put color in their skin before they were sold. They were graded based on their condition: #1, a "fancy" hen with a good large breast; #2, a thinner breast; CB, crooked breast bone; rejects, thin not much meat; hypo, no meat, egg-bound or water bellies.

During the Depression, when people were going under, my job was to collect chickens from farmers who owed money to the feed mill. It was a tough thing to do. The women would be crying. In some cases I'd pick the chickens up, pay Hunt and Behrens with my own money, then I'd take most of the birds back and put them in the houses. I lost nothing; I didn't get paid right away but I'd get a little all the time. There were no jobs, they had no other way to make a living. They would start buying grain again from Hunt and Behrens, but the slate was clean.

I raised rat terriers. When we moved the colony houses on my father's place, the rats would jump up. They'd been living under the floors. Then the rat terriers would go to work. The older dogs would train the younger ones.

Walter Soernsen

THE POULTRY CULLING WIZARD

Henry Graff was the man they chose to design a modern hatchery and install Mr. Byce's new gas incubators. Only a few miles north of Petaluma and with a capacity of 40,000 eggs, the Stony Point facility was a showplace. The Farm Advisor admired its modern layout and sturdy wire-fenced yards. Newspaper articles called Graff, a much-respected hatcheryman, "The Poultry Culling Wizard," famous for being fast and accurate at sorting out spent hens, having processed 250,000 birds in a 17-month period.

Born in 1866 into a family of German descent in Minnesota, Henry Graff was only nine months old when his father, a doctor, was killed, thrown from a buggy drawn by a runaway horse.

Henry's mother knew something of medicine from her husband. She once saved a Sioux chieftain from death during a blizzard. Little Crow crawled to her home, goes the family story, in the midst of a howling blue norther, hungry and frostbitten. She fed him grütze—eggs, milk and flour mixed with honey. When the tribesmen arrived to rescue their leader, they offered to massacre the family, but Little Crow forbade it and sent them to bring food for the household.

Henry started a diary when he was 18 years old; 12 leather bound journals survive. The entry for July 5, 1892 is "Elopeing with Annie." He spends July 7, 8 and 9th "Resting on till the old folks get over there thair rage." Annie was Anna Rieke.

In 1893 he writes, "I have a thermometer now so the severe heat and cold will be given."

A few years later the entry is

> Henceforth I shall study music
> all stormy days
> and whenever I have time.
> It will be on the violin.

February 20, 1895: "My baby boy born." He has three children in all. Five years later the first week in February is spent "Watching over my sick children, light snow fall." Later, in 1900, Henry Graff brings his family west. They leave San Francisco on the steamer *Gold* at 3:00 in the afternoon and arrive in Petaluma that night. Two days later they buy property.

"Our intention is to make California our home. We came here to benefit the health of our children, and purchased 18 acres of land 2 1/4 miles from Petaluma. Our future home if the children keep well."

[Daughter Ida Graff McDaniel lived to be 90. Her account is on page 8]

Graff pursues several aspects of the poultry industry. He experiments with A.R. Coulson to perfect chicken feed, sells high grade fowl for breeding purposes, and hatching eggs to Must Hatch and "to other exacting hatcheries that demand only the best posssible strains." His published biography describes him as a planner and builder of "model poultry ranches, including Clarence H. Dangers' Leghorn Ranch . . . the largest and most modern poultry ranch in the Petaluma vicinity and which contains sixteen 504–egg 'Petaluma' incubators," . . . and new, well built chicken houses "in marked contrast with many wherein the owners apparently believe that any old buildings are good enough."

April 18, 1906: "Earthquake 5:15 o'clock AM." A few days later, "Santa Rosa and San Francisco in ruins." The following year he is manager of Dangers' Ranch.

Graff's life is one of solid success; he serves on the grand jury, judges shows, culls flocks, and brings his favorite reporters freshly caught salmon and elk from his Mendocino County hunting lodge. He is active and well-known in the community and is regularly written up in the *Argus-Courier*.

L ater Henry has a hatchery business with a capacity of 40,000 eggs. He was "the first to use the then newly patented Must Hatch Incubators invented by A.E. Bourke and also used the first model gas incubator of Byce's Petaluma Incubator Company." Graff imported White Leghorn eggs from pure stock in the eastern United States.

January, 1950 contains two final entries. "Feeling quite bad this week" and "I just can't record temp now." Two years later he is dead at 86.

Henry Graff's journals

BY THEA LOWRY

COURTESY OF GRANDSON HERB GRAFF

HENRY GRAFF AND HUGH DANGERS AT THE NEWLY COMPLETED
WHITE LEGHORN RANCH, 1907. COURTESY HERB GRAFF.

600 TONS OF MILO

I worked for the Poultry Producers. We got price quotations from the Grain Exchange in Chicago twice a day by telephone to our headquarters in San Francisco. There was feed for chicks and for laying hens. We used to mix our own feeds, bran, milo, corn, wheat, shorts. Wheat and corn came from the Midwest in railroad cars, 60 tons per car.

Tons of milo came up from the Delta on barges; the barges had to come up the river, wait for the tide. They carried 600 tons of grain, sometimes got stuck in the mud. They'd be pulled by tugs. Those tug captains knew what they were doing. When the Washington Street drawbridge went up to let a tug and barge through, there was barely room, only inches to spare. Then they'd wait for the tide, to go back again.

The barges were unloaded by our conveyer belt. Augers on the barge brought the grain up from the hold and into the pit alongside the track. My job was to keep track of the railroad cars, their numbers and where they came from.

The mill was set up to handle grain and mix in bulk. The whole thing was a complicated procedure. We all worked hard. It was a disgrace to make a mistake.

Anonymous Contributor

VACCINATION DAY

Ye purchased the chicken ranch in 1946. My father-in-law, my husband Ted, our four children and I soon learned that the chicken business was not as lucrative as we had been led to believe. We had to learn to save in every way possible. We learned that chickens get sick.

We decided to vaccinate our own chickens for Newcastle disease and coccidiosis. We'd buy unsexed, day-old chicks. Saved money that way. When they reached an age where cockerels could be identified, we spent a Saturday separating them—the cockerels going into finishing batteries in the barn, the pullets into a small chicken house nearby. Here they lived for three more weeks, eating, drinking, resting and growing.

Then it was time for vaccinations. Every family member had a chore. I had two bottles of vaccine and two wire bristle devices. Ted and I shooed the pullets into a movable cage. He'd grab the bird by her legs and upend her, exposing her vent. The pullet reacted by frenzied wriggling and loud squawking, but with deft strokes, learned after only a few tries, I made three passes with the vaccine-bearing brush inside the vent, pressing hard enough to draw blood. The struggling pullet generally retaliated with a wild squirt of liquid feces.

Quickly, Ted would grab a wing and present the web to me. With the two sharp needles of the other device, I introduced the other vaccine. Ted then shoved her into the "catching box," a wooden crate with a movable slat opening in the top. This is repeated 300 times, with time-outs for a cup of coffee, a cigarette or a trip to the bathroom. Besides this dirty, demanding job, we have to gather the noon eggs, have lunch, rest, gather the evening eggs, clean and pack them before supper time.

Many unpleasant things connected with life at King's X Ranch have been erased from my memory, thank goodness, but not vaccination.

Our treatment worked, however, the pullets did not develop the dread diseases, but lived long, happy lives and graciously laid many eggs for us.

Helen F. King   See also pages 45 and 47.

Poehlmann Hatchery's blood testing crew included Ted Shepherd, Ralph Hobbs and Howard Hansen. Petaluma Museum Photo.
See account on page 70.

SIX BROTHERS IN THE POULTRY BUSINESS

In 1910, when he was 16, my father, Henry T. Bundesen, came to America. His family was from the Island of Langeness, a German island off the Danish coast. He was one of six brothers, each of whom immigrated when he was 16 to enter the poultry business. Many of the Petaluma poultry farmers were Germans, Danes and Swedes. A lot of Japanese were also in the business, but not so many Italians or Portuguese; they were mostly in the dairy business.

After establishing himself, my father went back to Föhr, Germany, and took a bride, Dora Feddersen. They came back and lived on Lohrman Lane near Straubville, named for a hatcheryman. I was born there in 1924 and grew up in the business. As children, we had to gather eggs and clean chicken houses; all very labor intensive as layer operations were. As farm kids, we couldn't play football, for instance, because of our after-school chores. The town kids seemed more affluent and their parents all usually spoke English, while the rural kids' parents often spoke their native language. The German community used to take one day off during the week, Wednesdays, and relax. We'd go up to the Russian River.

After high school, I was in military service and then went to college. In 1948 I took a degree in poultry science at Cal Poly. They taught me a lot about genetics, nutrition, incubation and poultry pathology. I came back to Petaluma and went into the hatchery business.

There were two industries here, meat birds and layers. It was probably 40/60 percent at first but later these proportions reversed. My family's business was breeding for meat birds. We obtained our foundation stock from one of the major suppliers, Christie and Nichols. These hens were the New Hampshire type originally sold as purebreds, then later crossed with the Cornish male which made for a large-breasted meat bird.

The chicken business underwent a metamorphosis similar to that of the turkey business when they went to white-feathered birds: everybody jumped on the bandwagon. Now producers went to White Rocks, and Arbor Acres was the primary breeder. Vantress Breeding Farm developed the male line. The hens carried the egg-laying capacity and the males passed on the characteristics of the heavy meat-bird male. Our hatchery produced baby chicks for the meat-bird industry and the egg industry.

Some Jewish, Chinese and other ethnic groups preferred their chickens to be prepared "New York dressed," which brought in a little more money. Not removing the head, feet and entrails seemed to intensify the flavor. There still is a market for this method, but regulators are wary of poultry which hasn't been eviscerated prior to sale.

After the War, California had to compete with Georgia, Arkansas, Mississippi—working with a much lower cost basis. The interstate highway system was starting and everyone got refrigerated trucks. Prices were high during WWII but later, because of the producers in the southeast, the industry had to integrate vertically. To eliminate each profit-taking layer, operators did their own hatching, feeding and processing. In those days it took 16 weeks to produce a four-pound fryer. Now it's less than half that time—seven weeks—to obtain a fryer of four pounds, two ounces, all because of advances in breeding and nutrition.

Consumer tastes have changed, too. Chicken used to be prepared for "company"; now it's considered modest fare. Chicken's useful yield is 70–72 percent, while beef is only 50–55 percent; but compare a cattle ranch: one person can oversee 200,000 fryers. The productive capacity of poultry is outstanding.

I believe the future lies in genetic engineering. Nowadays chickens live longer because of the better sanitation possible in the wire-floor cages. On the ground, we lost many, many more. Today's high production figures come from animals in perfect health. Poultry longevity is a miracle, not an aberration. And all from changes in methods which prevent infections and promote healthy birds.

About 1950 we purchased the Petaluma Hatchery from L.W. Clark and later changed the name to Bundesen Hatchery. We closed the hatchery in 1963. I'm in real estate now.

INTERVIEW BY THEA LOWRY

Herbert Bundesen

READY FOR THE MINK MAN

I worked for Sales and Bourke Hatchery from about 1956 to 1960. They became H&N Hatchery during that time, for Art Heisdorf and Nelson. They gave the trade name Nick Chick to the stock they developed. [The breeders' term "nick" means breeds true, passes on the desired characteristics.–Ed.] It lost its tail feathers early; its behind would be bare, an ugly looking bird, but it was a good layer.

Mortenson Hatchery on Baker Street produced the Honneger chick. Honneger chickens were lazy, wouldn't get out of each other's way. The chickens would pile up when you tried to move them; would just huddle and smother, whereas KimberChicks, from Niles, California, were very excitable. They'd be up in the rafters when you opened the door of the chicken house. No way that you could sneak up on them.

Then there's the Australorpe, which is black, and the White Leghorn cross. This produces a mean bird. When I was a kid, my uncle kept these in House Number Seven and he'd send me down to pick up the eggs. I had to roll down my sleeve to reach under the hen. She'd peck. The name of the cross was Austrawhite. Except for one or two black feathers, she was white. This wasn't a successful breed because their eggs were creamy in color and the public wanted only white eggs.

My job at the hatchery was to dispose of the cockerels after the sexors got through. My boss wanted the males disposed of immediately after being sexed to prevent somebody from starting a breeding farm with the H&N strain. I was to put them into a garbage can right away and put the lid on, but the mink man, who came at one o'clock, wanted the chicks freshly dead. He had a truck with a steel lined bed; we dumped the dead chicks in his truck. He took them to his farm in Schellville, where he ground them up for his minks.

Between these two considerations, on a big hatchery day, I had to work like hell; I'd fill six or eight garbage cans and would be putting the lid on the last one just as the mink man came.

On the other hand, the hatchery would give a bonus of cockerel chicks to its trusted customers to be raised to eat. A dozen or so, if they were wanted, for each hundred chicks.

Tim Talamentes   PHOTO OF A SCAVENGER TRUCK ON PAGE 94

EGGS AGAINST THE LIGHT

I came to Petaluma from Minnesota in 1935. At first I supported myself working at Woolworth's in San Rafael, and then I learned to candle eggs at Nye and Nissen. In 1937, I came to Poultry Producers of Central California where I candled eggs until the last nine years, when I had become an inspector.

Four lines of candlers each with an inspector worked at PPCC. Each girl worked (sorted) into a carton holding a dozen eggs, and would put three dozen at a time onto a conveyer belt, tagging each carton with her name and the count of how many of each grade of eggs she had found in each lot. A lot was one rancher's delivery of eggs.

The candler looks at the egg against a light in a black box-like arrangement, painted white inside and containing a mirror and a magnifying glass. The candler held two eggs in each hand and rolled them in such a way as to see the inside. Working quickly, she must sort out those with blood spots or breaks in the shell, look for the size of the air cells which determine freshness, and grade them for overall size, cleanliness and quality.

When I became an inspector, progress changed the system at the packing house and women no longer had to lift the heavy wooden cases from the ranches each holding 30 dozen eggs. Men now lifted the cases and usually helped to turn them as well.

The rancher was paid for the grade of eggs in his lot. My job as inspector was quality control of the candlers' work. Candlers were paid piecework wages at 50 cents a case. At one time we had 207 candlers and also many miscellaneous workers. Inspectors were paid at the rate of the highest paid candler plus 10 cents an hour.

During World War II we worked nine-hour days and some Saturdays, standing on our feet all day. During the war, one of the soldiers out at Two Rock had a chicken he wanted killed, which I did for him, but I thought to myself, "How can we win this war if soldiers can't even kill a chicken?"

During the War I met Vernon Vogle, who became my husband, at one of the USO dances in Petaluma. He was also stationed out at Two Rock.

Verna Hogberg Vogle

ILLUSTRATION PAGE 112.

PHOTO BY RUSSELL LEE C.1941 FOR THE FARM SECURITY ADMINISTRATION.
COURTESY OF THE LIBRARY OF CONGRESS.

WE TENDED TO HATE CHICKENS

In 1947-49, when I was in high school, I worked for Hardin Hatchery, earning 85 cents an hour instead of the 60 cents paid by most places. I was on the blood testing crew which went from farm to farm, testing chickens for BWD (bacillary white diarrhea). I'd get up at 4 AM to go to the hatchery, load the truck with coops and a special table sectioned off with slides (glass microscope plates) and be on our way. We'd go to the large chicken houses, herd the chickens out to cages in which we categorized them. There were heating lamps under the table. We'd hold a chicken on the table after nicking it under the wing, get blood on the slide, where the heat congealed it. Then we'd test the blood. Diseased chickens were separated from the flock and later destroyed. Healthy chickens were then let loose in the chicken yard.

Hardin Hatchery also had a rooster ranch on Hardin Lane were we dewattled the roosters to keep them from pecking each other. After cutting off the wattles, we'd toss them on on the ground where the roosters then gobbled them up.

Sometimes after our blood-testing the farmer would invite us down to his spring house where he'd pour us a big glass of his wonderful homemade wine. I refer to this period of my life as "chicken manure, wattles and wine."

To control lice we put "Black Leaf-40" (a tobacco substance) on the rear end of the chickens. It seemed to permeate the chicken and was effective in ridding the chickens of lice. We tended to hate chickens so once in a while in a mean streak we'd put the "Black Leaf-40" right on their anuses just to hear them squawk and run around.

Jim Harris

CHAMPION CHICKEN PLUCKER

My father came from Sicily. He stowed away on a ship at age nine, jumped ship at New Orleans, and wound up working on a dairy farm in Inverness where Mary Rogers, who became his wife and my mother, was also working.

My father sold dressed birds to the San Francisco market. He killed the chicken with a couple of knife thrusts in the head and then dry-plucked them, putting tail and wing feathers in one barrel and the soft feathers in gunny sacks. These were sold to pillow manufacturers in San Francisco. We sold the chicken blood to a fertilizer plant in Petaluma.

In 1922 my father entered the chicken picking contest at the county fair. He saw someone start to get ahead of him. He told me, "I spit out my cigarette and won the contest." That same year I was in the Egg Day Parade representing Pepper School sitting in a coop on the back of a flatbed truck.

Frank Faraone

GUILOU'S RANCH : GONE TO GRAPES

The ranch was 180 acres at the corner of Wilson Road and Windsor Road in Windsor. It was in poultry operation from 1915 to 1943, when my parents, Rene and Frances Guilou, sold it. It's now in grapes. The home movie [at the Petaluma Museum] was filmed in 1928.

By *G. D. Thomsen*

FRENCH~PORTUGUESE ANCESTORS

My great-grandfather, whose name was Coehlo, came from the Azores. When he got to California he checked the soil around where the Mark Hopkins Hotel in San Francisco is now and pronounced it unfit to grow potatoes. He came to Petaluma and purchased land which is still in the family. He changed his name to King.

My father's family name was Suares. They came from Portugal and changed the name to Suez. My father lived out his life on the same ranch on Marshall Avenue where he was born. His name was William J. Suez.

My mother, Odette Cayla, was French-born. Her mother had immigrated alone from the Decazeville—a region in southern France—to San Francisco and found a job at the Palace Hotel and sent for her family. Later they moved to Petaluma where my grandfather Cayla worked for the railroad. My mother worked for a confectionery and at the silk mill. After my father returned from the war in Europe they were married. She was only 19.

My father worked for Hilderbrand and others as a candler for many years and, because he had to stand all day, at night his legs ached. Eventually he shifted to picking up eggs from the ranches.

By *Laurette Suez Brindley*

JUST LIKE BABIES

My parents were born in Holland in 1866 and purchased the 30 acres in Petaluma in 1900. My father built the house, a barn and colony houses for the chickens. We had about 2,000. Our chores, as children on a ranch, were to milk the cows, pull the kale, and haul feed for the cows with a horse and sled.

I married Henry Filippini in 1927 and we bought five acres adjoining my parents' property during the Depression. I had a brooder house of my own with two coal oil lamps, good for 500 chicks. If the chicks were too warm, they spread out. If they got to close to the lamps they were cold. "A chilled chick is a dead one," we said. If they got too close to each other, they'd smother. I'd raise the wick of the lamp to give more heat. You get them chilled once, you're done.

You could raise every chick. I watched them. I went to see them before I went to bed. If all was well they made a nice circle around those lamps.

One time I went to get the chicks from the Must Hatch Hatchery and saw a fire on the way home, wondered what it was....it was *my* brooder house. One of the kerosene lamps I lighted to warm the room for the chicks before I left had exploded.

I brought the chicks in their boxes into our bedroom and kept them there for three weeks. My husband built a new brooder house for me, putting in an electric brooder, for my next batch of chicks.

I would spread opened grain sacks on the floor under the brooder, to catch the droppings. When they were soiled I would put the sacks on the fence, spray them with a hose and let them dry in the sun. The chicks have to be kept clean, you know, just like babies.

Anna Weiling Filippini

MAX POEHLMANN IN FRONT OF THE HATCHERY.
PHOTO COURTESY ED MANNION COLLECTION.

FLEAS IN THE BASEMENT, RATS IN THE BARN

My husband, Donald G. Hadley, and I were married in October, 1932. We moved 12 times that year because of the Depression; there were very few jobs.

My husband's grandfather, George V. McGlauflin, had a small ranch on Jewett Road in Petaluma with 2,000 chickens, a horse named Jack and a cow. We helped Grandpa Mac with plowing, chores and housework and we enjoyed fresh eggs, churned butter, garden vegetables and lovely, plump boysenberries with cream from Bossy.

Our next job was out beyond Washoe House on a ranch with free range chickens belonging to Billy McCarter. He supplied fertile eggs to the hatcheries in Petaluma. The chickens, not being confined, got to roam around the pasture and pick greens and eat bugs, making them very healthy. We shared the old ranch house with another couple and also took care of about a dozen cows which had to be milked twice a day. The milk was sold to a creamery and also fed to the chickens with the mash.

Then we got another job on a ranch off Gossage Avenue owned by Maximillian Mordecai Rosenblum. We were provided a small cottage and $50 a month wages. I was to clean eggs from 8,000 hens. We used a shoe buffer with a strip of emery paper fastened over the wool to clean the manure off the eggs. Then I packed them in a carton and they next went to two candlers, who examined them for blood spots, and those were sold to bakeries at a reduced price. The packing and candling was done in the basement under the Rosenblum house. This cellar had an infestation of fleas. My legs were covered with bites as I stood there working. After I complained, the place was sprayed and it was better for a while.

My husband's job was the never-ending one of cleaning the manure from the chicken houses, spraying them and scrubbing out the wooden troughs each day and refilling them and keeping the feeders full. My husband made up the mash, according to Mr. R.'s prescription, in the big barn in back of the main house. It was so rat-infested that they ran all over the place whenever the light was turned on. The dog could kill at least a dozen before the rats went into hiding.

R osenblum had a huge horse that pulled the manure wagon. The harness was broken in many places and badly patched with wire. The horse was unable to back up and would always fall down when he tried.

One day I came upon a broody hen sitting with her feathers all fluffed up, resolute in her determination to raise a family. I picked her up and received the usual fierce pecking. The brood of babies that she'd been trying to mother was a litter of newborn kittens, mewing and squeaking in bewilderment.

On this job we kept working after dark, culling hens, because they were easy to catch when they were roosting. We identified sick chickens by their small, pale combs, and we checked each hen for age by feeling the width of the pelvic bones. Culls were loaded into wire crates on the old truck and Mr. R. would take them to San Francisco to sell to restaurants, along with eggs that were broken in the processing. These were dumped into a large can, strained to remove shells and dirt, and sold to bakeries.

The work was exhausting but jobs were scarce. We stayed on.

The food was pretty awful: creamed corn beef on toast and canned vegetables; peanut butter mixed with tomato soup on bread for lunch. Once in a while Mr. R. gave us some cottage cheese, and I made jam when the berries ripened.

A new man came along and I was told to feed him and charge him board. One day he asked if we ever had meat. I said no, we couldn't afford it. Later that evening he brought me two nice chickens. I asked no questions and he said nothing.

By *Stella E. (Neal) Hadley*

SCAVENGER TRUCK IN 1930, FROM FILES OF THE FARM ADVISOR.
COURTESY DR. FRANCINE A. BRADLEY, AVIAN SCIENCES, UC-DAVIS.

CROW, CLUCK, CACKLE AND SING

In 1902, Penngrove poultryman Al Hermann looked after a thousand fowls on the William Evart ranch. Hermann was locally famous for teaching the birds tricks. He had roosters that would "scrap on command, and hens that respond to their names and come to him when called." One hen did a half-dozen tricks, but the most remarkable thing was Hermann's ability to imitate the voices of all kinds of fowls. "For nine years he made a study of this and can now imitate the music of every kind of fowl, from the gobbler to the duck and from the tiny bantam to the huge Brahma." Contemporary accounts in newspapers stated that he was widely renowned "for his ability to crow, cluck, cackle and sing."

Hermann was born in San Francisco on September 11, 1876 and was self-supporting from age eight. He didn't finish the second grade, but became a carpenter at age 12. According to a published biographical sketch, in 1894 at the age of 18, he walked from San Francisco to Penngrove to begin work on a chicken ranch.

In 1904 he married Tillie Behrens, daughter of Emil and Louise Nisson Behrens, and they had two daughters. He spent the later years of his life as a building contractor but continued to entertain with his avian imitations. A recording of the cackles and crows of some 28 different birds, now in the Ed Mannion History Collection, was made from a radio broadcast around 1950 when Hermann was about 75.

THEA S. LOWRY

SEVEN CARS, SEVEN DAYS A WEEK

During the peak hatching season, from the middle of February to the first of June, up to seven Railway Express cars left Petaluma every day of the week carrying commercial chicks to egg producers all over California. Thirty-nine hatcheries were in business in those days, they say.

My father-in-law was D.B. Walls, a poultry breeder and a co-founder of Poultry Producers and the Egg Laying Contest. At one time, all the hatcheries in Petaluma used his bloodlines. For many years he was highly successful. He thought the poultry industry would go on and on as he had always known it and that eventually his interests would come to his daughter Barbara and me.

But the industry changed almost overnight and caught him by surprise. Large breeding organizations with strong financial backing and the skills of hired geneticists developed. Two major breeders of seed corn, Pioneer out of Iowa and DeKalb from Illinois, went into poultry. Another scientific breeder was John Kimber of Niles (now a part of Fremont, in southern Alameda County.) He started out small and became widely known, and eventually his company sold out to DeKalb.

Art Heisdorf was a geneticist for Kimber in the late 1940s. He left Kimber to establish his own breeding business, known as Heisdorf and Nelson Farms, in Kirkland, Washington. In 1953 Heisdorf started a breeding farm and hatchery in Riverside, California, followed by one in Turlock in '54 or '55 and then, in 1957, he bought out Sales and Bourke Hatchery here in town. It had been a franchised hatchery of Heisdorf and Nelson. Poehlmann Hatchery was franchising Hy-Line chicks from Des Moines, Iowa.

Producers were paying attention to chicks' nickability—a term that became popular at that time—meaning the ability to breed true, pass on the desired characteristics. D.B. Walls' bloodline was for large birds which had been what the public wanted. These birds weighed up to six pounds and could be sold for meat. Producers liked them because they would fetch 35 to 50 cents a pound. The Campbell Soup people, for one, would buy worn-out fowl.

But then commercial [table] egg production, as opposed to small ranch production, appeared in the late '40s and '50s. The big breeders were producing small birds, appropriate for cage operations. These birds had good livability, lower feed consumption and good laying capacity. They were not buying from D.B. Walls.

This phenomenon seemed to happen overnight in the mind of the small breeder. To change over would require a big capital investment. I was working for Walls in 1955 when he was 66 years old. We didn't have the space for the new kind of breeding farm and he didn't want to borrow the money. The age of the small breeder was over.

Bill Murch

WE'D LEAVE FIVE MINUTES

My father was Sam Fishman and my mother was Sarah Krantz. They were both from Poland, and married there in 1913. He was trained as a locksmith and came that same year to Minneapolis to join his brother. There was big industry there because of the railways. My father worked as a journeyman machinist on the building of locomotives.

The Jews were being driven from their homes in Poland; my mother traveled through Siberia, China and Japan to arrive in Seattle in 1917, on her way to join my father.

In 1917, World War I, there were plenty of locomotives but they needed ships. Sam left the railroad and came to San Francisco to work in the shipyards. Then the war ended and so did the jobs. All the shipyard workers—Danes, Germans, my father and mother—came to Petaluma, to the chicken business.

My father did day-work for a year or two on other people's ranches, managed a chicken ranch for an absentee owner for a while, and then bought his own place on Chapman Lane, five acres. Everything was divided into five acre lots. This was 1921 or '22. I was the second oldest of their five children.

In 1931, when egg prices were low, my father couldn't get enough to pay his feed bill. The Golden Eagle Milling Company came in and foreclosed. But my father knew the law. When they came to get the chickens, he pointed out that they couldn't take them without a court order and the law allowed a two week delay. It was illegal to take personal property—100 chickens, a cow, a horse—to settle a debt. But some creditors would come in the middle of the night and take the cow, the tools. The farmer would get up in the morning and find all his chickens gone. In due time they took all our chickens, except the 100.

My father became very ill and his weight dropped from 180 to 135 pounds. He was diagnosed with ulcers, but recovered after treatment and lived to be 86.

We were fortunate in that the man who sold us the ranch held the mortgage. From 1931 to 1936, we paid no interest and nothing on the principal, only insurance and taxes.

We had eggs, milk, butter and a garden. In the two weeks' delay, before the chickens were removed, we sold the eggs and kept the money, probably two or three hundred dollars. There wasn't much in the bank.

In 1932, my father bought a new Ford truck, a 1½-ton flatbed, with a 40 horsepower engine. He hauled grain from the Valley—barley, wheat, oats sometimes—and delivered directly to the ranches.

In 1936, my brother Morris, who was in FFA, [in Bart Reardon's high school ag class] had a project of 2,000 meat bird chicks. He made quite a bit of money. We thought we would go into heavy meat birds, Rhode Island Reds. We were the first in the county to go solely into meat birds.

We went to the Marin School out at the end of Western Avenue and to high school in town. On Saturday, at the football game, we'd leave five minutes before the half, feed the chickens, and then rush back to watch three quarters of the last half. We could get it done—there were three of us, my brothers Morris and Julius and me. We drove a 1925 Oldsmobile touring car.

Early in 1937, I went to Los Angeles and met with the owner of our property. We wanted to refinance. He settled five or six years' interest for half, plus the principal, which was two or three thousand dollars.

Sol Fishman

THE LANGUAGE OF THE HOME COUNTRY

My father was Nathan Silver and my mother was known as Ali. Her maiden name was Yehoved Bragar. Yehoved was the woman who wet-nursed Moses, who parted the waters of the Red Sea.

My parents escaped from Bolshevik Russia and lived on the East Coast for six years. Then they came to my father's sister's ranch in Cotati. He'd been emotionally traumatized and needed a quieter life. They moved to the ranch on Woodward Avenue in Penngrove—five acres—in 1928 or '29.

About the time that Roosevelt came in, my father had to sell the poultry. The sheriff came and sat on our place so that the money collected went to the feed supplier and the hatchery.

Then my father went out and worked. He sold rice hulls and hay, and he bought and sold hens. He had a plant and sold dressed chickens, to accounts mostly in San Francisco.

He purchased an old typewriter which I learned to use to do his business papers. I was about 12. I sometimes went with my father when he delivered hens. Sometimes I drove truck for him.

My parents spoke the language of the home country to each other, but usually not to my brother and me. They wanted to learn English and as a result my mother and I learned to read together. My father taught us to love this country.

They went out of business in 1958 or so. It was no longer feasible to make a living. The market price for chickens in this area was the same that you paid for dressed chickens.

Charlotte Silver Goldstein

WHAT WE COULD CARRY

My parents were Kisuke and Tamano Kai. They were married in Japan, in the state of Hiroshima, and they came to the United States in 1918. They worked as laborers in the hop fields and in the apple driers. They pruned apple and prune trees in the orchards, each time in a different location in Sonoma County. There were other Japanese working here in the same way.

The farmers provided housing, so there was always a roof over our heads, a kitchen, and a bedroom, though sometimes it was just a lean-to against a big barn. As laborers my parents made three different moves a year, consequently it could be three different schools for the children. It was hard on a child.

I was born in August, 1920, in Sebastopol. When I was ready to go to school, my parents wanted to send me to one school. They were able to buy property in the name of my sister and me. They could set up an estate for their minor daughters. We were citizens since we were born here.

We moved to Penngrove in October, 1926, and I attended Eagle School (now Penngrove), then brand-new, and continued in Penngrove schools for nine years.

Mother picked me up every afternoon so I could help with the eggs. She started driving in 1926. My father suffered a minor accident and was never interested in driving again. Mother was one of the very few Japanese women that drove at that time. We had a Model A Ford.

When I was in high school, I didn't get home on the bus

until 5 PM. We were on the first run in the morning. We left before 8 and we were on the last bus out. But the eggs were waiting for me to do.

Sometimes after school I'd be so hungry I'd spend a nickel on a hamburger at McAninch's, across from the high school.

The chicken business was every day of the year. No off days, no holidays. If we went anywhere, we had to come home by 4 PM at the latest. I went to one football game during my three years in high school.

We had 7.76 acres on Goodwin Avenue. There were six or eight Japanese poultry farmers in our immediate area, Elysian and Goodwin Avenue. There were others in the Penngrove area, on the east side, also the Corona area, between Old Adobe and Ely. There were more out in the Skillman area.

Our capacity in laying hens was around 10,000. I think we were about middle capacity. Many other Japanese and Japanese-American families had larger capacity.

We sold our empty sacks to the sack buyer and fertilizer to the fertilizer buyer. We sold our scrubby chickens to the chicken buyer, whose name was Obert. The money we made paid for our living expenses. Checks from the eggs went into the business account, paying for feed, chicks, utilities and the mortgage. We built this house in 1940-41.

We sold eggs to Nye and Nissen, Casperson and Sons and others. We were never members of the Poultry Producers.

We had a Sunday School where we went to learn Japanese; a Community Center for New Year's Eve parties and picnics and Boy Scouts. It folded up in the '30s.

When the War started, it was nothing like, "You get out in

24 hours" as it was for the Japanese around Seattle. At first it was only the Coast they cleared the Japanese from, and we thought to buy a motor home and go to Yuba City. But then it was said that all Japanese in California were to be relocated.

Pearl Harbor was in December [1941]. We began selling our property in April, but others sold before that and were not treated fairly. Sam Nisson, from whom we bought feed, worked with the business people to get fair prices. He got other ranchers to buy our feed and chickens. Sam said we had to get good renters for our house, and he did. He had power of attorney to act for us and he put the rent into our bank account. Then, after we were gone, he rented our chicken houses as well.

Sam Nisson lived in Lakeville and was the owner of Corona Feed Mill. He helped his Japanese customers.

We left in May, 1942, by train from the Santa Rosa Depot. Most of the Sonoma, Mendocino and Napa County Japanese, and perhaps Marin, too, left when we did; half of them on Saturday, the others on Sunday.

All we could take was what we could carry, including bedding. Everything else went into two rooms, one in the house and one in the barn. They were padlocked. When we returned after three years, we found the locks still in place. Others were not so lucky.

There were Caucasians living in our houses during the war, so there was no burning of our houses. But the Community Center was burned.

We went to the Merced Fairgrounds. In the fall of 1942, we were moved inland to Granada, Colorado, close to the Kansas border.

I always took it that we were safe. There was barbed wire and guards up in the towers. We had food, each other, we had movies. I felt safe.

The Army reopened the West Coast before the end of the war. Sam Nisson, who had kept in touch with us, suggested we return to see our place before we made up our minds to return. I came, alone, then returned to the camp to tell my parents that we should come home.

I was married in camp, and my husband and I came here a couple of months before my parents came.

We stayed in the poultry business until the early 1950s.

Mary Kai Nakagawa

The "PRIDE of PETALUMA" BROODER STOVE
————Latest Fresh Air Model————

1917 ADVERTISEMENT FOR "PRIDE OF PETALUMA" FRESH AIR BROODER STOVE FACTORY, J.E. KRESKY, PROPRIETOR. ~ COURTESY PETALUMA MUSEUM.

CHICKENS RUNNING AROUND

My parents and my eldest sister were both born in Japan. I was born in Hawaii in 1905. I'm the first son and third child of ten.

We came here because my mother wanted to raise chickens. They were living on my father's vineyard in Tulare County, and she already had about a hundred chickens just running around picking up food on their own. I was in high school when my family came to the Petaluma area in 1923.

Our first place was a little farm on the other side of Penngrove. It was already set up as a chicken ranch. The only thing is, the old man who was there didn't care for raising chickens anyway, so he had chickens running around. We thought, with our limited experience in chickens, that we didn't need any chicken houses. We'd had chickens running all around before. When it rained they'd go in the shed where we used to keep horses. A hundred and something chickens didn't need too much room. That's all, we were thinking, a few hundred chickens. But when we got here, a few hundred chickens meant nothing.

Feed dealers gave us some advice and they loaned us the money that we needed. My father soon found out that everything wasn't so easy, because feed houses, when they want their money, they come and try to get it any way.

I found a job in Sebastopol working in apples and moved there. I used to go back and forth to visit my father. I worked and went to school and graduated in January, 1925. My parents were deeply in debt and couldn't make it at that farm, but then we found this place on Willow Avenue, south of Cotati, and collaborated with the owner and his son in getting started in the business and building some chicken houses.

I met my future wife, Sawame, when she was about 17. She was born in Santa Rosa in 1912. Her father was Ichizo Furuta, a grocer there since before the earthquake. His goods were brought from San Francisco by buckboard [horse and wagon] or by train. He supplied food to the boarding houses for Japanese workers in the hop fields around Healdsburg and Windsor.

L ater on the Furutas gave up the grocery store and went into raising strawberries. During the influenza epidemic in 1918, they quit the ranch and moved to Fountain Grove where they lived with Kanaye Nagasawa [successor to and adopted heir of Thomas Lake Harris, the founder of the utopian community there, who died in 1906]. Her father was educated and fluent in Japanese and acted as a scribe for Kanaye Nagasawa. They stayed there until about 1928 living in the house below the big round barn.

We met in Sebastopol and got married in 1929. After our first child was born we lived here at the ranch with my mother and sister. My mother lived with us until she died. It is the Japanese custom for the eldest son to look after the parents and get the property, if he's shown that he's responsible. I helped my brother get established with 3,000 pullets on a place on North Petaluma Boulevard.

W e really struggled but we were quite in debt in the Depression. The feed dealers—McNear, Golden Eagle and the Crowleys—attached the ranch, but we continued to stay and work; they gave us $500 a month to live on. We finally paid them off and everything was all right. Everybody was helping, everybody pitched in.

Then the war came. We were relocated. They didn't give us much time. We left everything here except what we could carry. We sold the chickens for 15 cents apiece. We were in Merced at first, and then we were sent to Granada, Colorado. In 1943, the government okayed the 442nd, a volunteer Japanese-American combat battalion, and at the same time the War Relocation Authority let some people leave for school or work.

I didn't want our children to grow up in that camp life. I was able to leave camp and check out places first and I chose Girard, Pennsylvania, a potato farm. The pay was 50 cents an hour, but we were very frugal and saved money, thanks to Sawame.

We stayed in Pennsylvania even after the war was over. Then we got a telegram that Sawame's mother was dying. We got a trailer and drove. All through the journey everyone was very nice to us. In Texas a grocery man came out of his store and welcomed us and we were so amazed. Later we found out that the Lost Battalion of Texas was saved by the 442nd in France.

When we got back here, everything was in good shape. Our house had been rented out while we were gone. Our neighbors were good friends who had kept us in touch. The feed store man checked the place. Still, there was a lot of work to be done and, before we could get anything off the ranch, to start the new flock, it cost us $18,000. We paid it off in about five years. We didn't splurge on anything. We never went on vacation until 1962 when we retired, then we took a trip to Japan. We had six children who all went to college. We've been retired for 30 years now.

Hideo Shimizu and Sawame Furuta Shimizu
INTERVIEW BY LUCY KORTUM

RAYMOND TRAVERS GERE, WITH PUPPY AND KITTEN, SURVEYS CASES CONTAINING 720 FRESH EGGS FROM HIS 2,000-LAYER RANCH IN HESSEL (1927). SEE PAGE 109.

MAKING A GO OF IT

These diary entries were written in January, 1923, by Raymond Travers Gere, born February 5, 1898. A student of poultry husbandry at UC-Davis' Department of Agriculture, he had just purchased six acres of untilled land ready for poultry farming in Hessel, California. He spent the next five months plowing, planting kale, building hen houses, purchasing chicks and equipment, and making preparations for his wedding to Janie Simpson Weir, 22, whose arrival he awaited with great eagerness.

Monday, January 1, 1923

Early fog, Then Warm & Fine   All Hail!   1923!

May you see much of happiness and a steadily better growing world. I start you working and was asleep when you came into being, in my little cot (with the hard lump) on the ex-Caldwell place, and now Gere place, here six miles south of Sebastopol.

I start you with high hopes—for one thing, that you will see Janie and I wedded & happy, and able to adjust ourselves before you're gone. Then I'm getting started on this place, & you'll see what success I have in raising & housing chicks and pullets, & making a go of it.

Health we have now, may it continue.

Thursday, Jan. 6, 1923

Rained all Night – Misty a.m.

Joined the Farm Bureau yesterday, through J.J. Irving. Wrote diary, looked over various things. Off to S.F. –waited an hour in Petaluma, & sketched expenses, roughly, for a year or two to come.

H & I discussed my money needs, & went over my plans & figures again. Will take $700 first 3 months – $350 for 2000 chix, $315 for 3 mos. feed; $40 for 2 tons coal, $80 for my eats, 4 mos; these are among the main items. Then to 7 months, when eggs laid begin to pay expenses, have about $400 more for feed to pay, $100 for grub, $100 wedding & house expenses, $1,300 outlay to 7 months.

Harry is lending it as I need it, borrowing on his stocks. It will be all out go until Sept. when pullets begin laying well. Last four months of year, can figure on $150 month average profit, if pullets do pretty well. Hope to get together $500 more to build a 500 unit laying house this summer to put the pullets in.—Counting my hens before they are raised?—have to do it, to reach a basis for figuring a way out.

Absorbed in my little interests these days, feathering the nest. Many interesting things going on in the world I do not record. Too small a space for world affairs – mine are so much more important (!)

Raymond Travers Gere

Raymond and Janie had four children: Dorie, Millie, Ray, Jr. and Bobby. Their second daughter wrote:

My sister was born in April of 1924 and I was born June 2, 1926. We lived in Hessel until I was three.… Dad would give us a ride in the masher which is a long tubular shaped vessel that hung on a pulley. We would go riding along with him as he would stop and give the mash to the chickens inside. Sometimes he would just give us a push and we would slide the length of the chicken house. That was a fun thing that I remember—and the wheelbarrow rides.

Mildred Weir Gere (Davis)
ACCOUNT PROVIDED BY HER DAUGHTER DIANE DAVIS-JAIGIRDAR
PHOTOS ON PAGES 4 AND 108

I TRADED MY SUSHI

I was born in 1920 on the Elphick Ranch in Penngrove, where I lived until I was seven. My father was renting it and raising chickens. My mother did the outside work looking after chicks, and I remember getting up on a chair to do the dishes. Then we moved to Skillman Lane and I used to have to handle all the cooking. My father would tell me what to make. He would get me an apple box to stand on to reach the stove.

We couldn't own the place on Skillman—aliens weren't allowed to purchase property. We had to buy a name. I think we bought the name Nakano, so our place was called Naka-no Farms. When my brother Jim came of age it was transferred to him.

My first teacher was Miss Gekkler. I went to the Eagle School, the new Penngrove School and then Wilson School. We ate lunch in the woodshed and I remember trading my sushi with you, Althea [Larsen Torliatt–see page 10], for your pot roast sandwich on brown bread....There were all different nationalities from the farms in the school so we had plenty in common.

My father used to take my brother Sam and me to town once a week and he'd give us each 50 cents to spend, big money in those days, to go get whatever we wanted. We'd go to the dime store and buy junk, buy ice cream, a big treat.

My father had about 20,000 chickens. As kids we did the work—feeding the chickens, gathering eggs, cleaning them until late at night. We were always wiping the eggs. We sold them to Ben Gold and Nye and Nissen. We bought feed from Golden Eagle.

When I was 22 I married George Masada. My husband worked for Senator William Rich of Marysville. We were relocated to Colorado during the war.

My mother got sick at camp, had a fever of 103 or 104 for three days. We took her to the dispensary, and the doctor said he would see her in a couple of days. We told him she was expiring. My dad said he was going to drive her to Denver. The doctor said, "I'll look at her on my day off." By the time his day off came, she was gone. We came home, and I remember my father holding the urn with her ashes on his lap all the way home in the car. She was only 50. My dad was so sad he died a year later.

When we got home our two dogs that we'd left four years before were ecstatic. Now my son Gary and his wife—both chemists—have two kids, and they speak in Spanish when they don't want us to understand.

Marlene Miyano Masada   INTERVIEW BY ALTHEA LARSEN TORLIATT

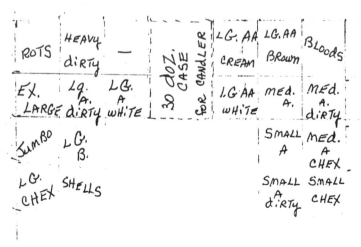

VERNA VOGLE SKETCHED THE LAYOUT OF THE BENCH FROM MEMORY.
ACCOUNT PAGE 85. COURTESY ED FRATINI.

SEAFARING MEN

*Conversation between "Icy" Helgason and
Captain Fred Klebingat
on Mason Street, San Francisco, in 1966.*

IH: That was a byword by a sailor—to go to Petaluma and raise chickens.

FK: You didn't have to work at all, just sell the eggs.

IH: To a seafaring man, thinking about retiring, it seemed an easy way to make a living. But it took a scientist.

FK: I saw so many skippers come back from Petaluma and go to sea to get something to eat.

IH: I talked to one. He told me if he knew as much when he went into the poultry business as when he got out, he would have been all right.

FK: You remember 'The Terrible Swede' in the Packers? He eventually got his chicken ranch. Up at Petaluma. And the next time I saw him he had no use for chickens: "Those sons-of-bitches! They climbed on top of each other and smothered to death. 1800 of them! Next night a thousand with their feet up. I had to buy oil to burn the god damn things!"

Captain Benneche of the *James Johnson*— he acknowledged that he had to go back to sea to get money to buy chicken feed.

"Icy" Helgason in 1962:

Every sailor those days...that's all you heard: chicken ranch! Just go around and pick up the eggs. The chicken ranch was a sailor's dream.

Captain Fred Klebingat again, in 1978:

Retiring on a farm —well, many Pacific Coast sailing skippers did just that. But I heard of only one who made it go—Henningsen. He was the skipper of the *Mary Winkelman* for quite a while.

A lot of seamen those days thought that life on a chicken ranch was the life of Riley. But most of them found out that they were dealing with the most ornery animal in the barnyard. There was more to it than picking up the eggs in the morning. Most of them went broke.

I spoke to Captain Dahlquist, one of the Charles Nelson Company skippers, when he quit the sea for a chicken farm. "If you see me at sea again," he said, "you can be sure the chickens need some chicken feed." I notice that he went back to sea.

Then there was Sutherland, "Silk Hat Harry," mate in the *Aryan* when she last left San Francisco, and in the *Falls of Clyde*. He quit the *Clyde* at Honolulu and went into chicken ranching in the Islands. "One is bound to make money," he said, "with eggs selling at a dollar a dozen." He went broke. And Harry was a man who was careful with his money. Harry later set up as a bootlegger in Oakland; that may have been more successful.

RECORDED BY *Karl Kortum*

FOR FURTHER READING

Petaluma's Poultry Pioneers is a companion volume to **Empty Shells**, an illustrated scrapbook of the poultry industry, scheduled next in the **Chicken Farm Chronicles** series. A collection of the contributors' original narratives for the current book, organized by Maxine Kortum Durney, is available in local libraries and at the Museum.

Readers who wish to learn more about Petaluma will enjoy Adair Heig's **History of Petaluma: A California River Town** (San Francisco, Scottwall Associates, 1982). For more specific information on the evolution of the industry, **Western Poultry History,** George Biddle, ed. (Modesto, Pacific Egg and Poultry Association, 1989) is thorough. Lewis A. Hillyard's detailed discussion, **Poultry Producers of Central California** (unpublished thesis, 1983) is available at Sonoma State University library. An overview of the business is covered in **American Poultry History 1823-1973,** Hanke *et al,* (American Poultry Historical Society, Madison, Wisconsin, 1973).

Kenneth Kann discusses the unique contribution of Jewish chicken ranchers in **Comrades and Chicken Ranchers: the Story of a California Jewish Community** (Cornell University Press, 1993). A biography of one rancher: **Joe Rappaport: The Life of a Jewish Radical** was published by Temple University Press in 1981.

ILLUSTRATIONS

INDEX

The Petaluma Museum Association

20 Fourth Street ~ Petaluma, California 94952 ~ [707] 778-4398

Designed and typeset by Thea S. Lowry
Printed by Barlow Printers

PETALUMA'S POULTRY PIONEERS

Published under the Auspices of

The Petaluma Museum Association

20 Fourth Street ~ Petaluma, California 94952
(707) 778-4398

_ _

Additional copies may be purchased
at the Petaluma Museum or by mail:

Make Check Payable to the Chicken House Project

Petaluma's Poultry Pioneers ISBN **0-96101116-0-2, $10.95**

Enclose $13.50 for each book (Includes tax, S & H)

Name_____

Address_____

City_____State____ZIP_____

Manifold Press ~ Box 1744 ~ Ross CA 94957

_ _

Additional copies may be purchased
at the Petaluma Museum or by mail:

Make Check Payable to the Chicken House Project

Petaluma's Poultry Pioneers ISBN **0-96101116-0-2, $10.95**

Enclose $13.50 for each book (Includes tax, S & H)

Name_____

Address_____

City_____State____ZIP_____

Manifold Press ~ Box 1744 ~ Ross CA 94957

NOTES